Legends from the NHL's Toughest Job

ABOUT THE AUTHOR

Stan Fischler is regarded as the dean of North American hockey writers. The prize-winning author has written more than 60 books on hockey. One of them, *The Hockey Encyclopedia,* which was co-authored with his wife, Shirley, is regarded as the bible of the sport. Fischler also writes a weekly column, *Inside Sports,* which has been carried for the past 20 years by the Toronto Star Syndicate. Among other publications which have carried his byline are *The New York Times, Sports Illustrated, Newsweek* and *The Village Voice.*

The versatile Fischler is also a prominent hockey broadcaster, having done analysis for 20 years. Stan has taught journalism at Columbia University, Fordham University, and Queens College.

A native of Brooklyn, Fischler lives in Manhattan with his wife and two children.

GOALIES

Legends from
the NHL's Toughest Job

STAN FISCHLER

W
Warwick Publishing Inc.
Toronto   Los Angeles

ISBN 1-895629-40-3

Published by Warwick Publishing Inc.
24 Mercer Street, Toronto, Ontario M5V 1H3

Distributed in the United States by:
Firefly Books Ltd.
250 Sparks Ave,
Willowdale, Ontario
M2H 2S4

Front Cover photo: Dan Hamilton, Vantage Point Studios
Cover design: Dave Hader/Studio Conceptions
Text design: Jacqueline Lealess
Editorial services provided by Word Guild, Toronto

Published in Canada by:
McGraw-Hill Ryerson Limited
300 Water Street
Whitby, Ontario
L1N 9B6

Printed and bound in Canada by Metropole Litho Inc.

Acknowledgements

The way goaltenders get help from their backchecking forwards and crease-clearing defensemen, goaltending historians require backup personnel to produce a book about the puckstopping profession.

And, to be sure, we got plenty of support at all ends of the writing rink.

From the opening face-off researcher-reporter aids David Levy and Susanna Mandel-Mantello provided critical interviews, insights, and editorial input. Without them, there would be no book.

Interns David Kolb, Kym Chevian, Craig Levitt, Joe Reynoso, Brendan McGovern and Stephanie Toskos delivered critical insights and corrections both in the office and the arenas and also were invaluable assistants.

A select group of reporters throughout the NHL delivered pungent interviews with a number of goalies. Hence, our thanks to Jim Ramsay, Rick Middleton, Brian McDonough, Keith Drabik, Harris Peet, Sandra MacPherson, Eric Martin, Wayne Geen, Al Goldfarb and Mary McCarthy.

None of this would have been possible without the ever-enthusiastic backing of McGraw Hill Ryerson publisher Don Broad, who not only relishes a good hockey game, but appreciates a great goaltender — and understood the need for a book about the same. To Don: Thanks, again!

Contents

Introduction

My respect for the goaltending business developed at a relatively early age. It was the winter of 1947-48, one of the coldest and snowiest in New York history.

Our roller hockey team, The Woodside Whippets, were "snowed out" of action and forced to find other diversions until our rink could be cleared of the heavy white stuff.

We did the natural thing and retired to Central Park in Manhattan, where an assortment of lakes and ponds had frozen to offer a dozen ice hockey rinks. The Whippets, who ranged between 13 and 15 years of age, couldn't have been happier.

There was only one problem: our regular goalie didn't show up and a substitute had to be found. Alas! This was the moment for which I had been waiting. Although I was left defenseman on the Whippets, I had a long yearning to play goal.

I can think of a dozen reasons, but suffice to say that the position had always fascinated me. Goalie pads were so big, so distinct and, I assumed, so protective. The challenge of me, the goalie, against the world also appealed to my independent instincts, and having worshipped Toronto netminder Turk Broda, I had all the incentive I needed.

What I didn't have was goalie pads. First of all, I was a defenseman and secondly, even if I wasn't, who could afford them in those Depression days? Certainly not the Fischler family.

When I learned I'd be in the nets that day, I did the next best thing. I ambled into my grandmother's kitchen and discreetly removed a pair of plastic cushions off the chairs. The cushions measured about two feet by two feet which meant that if I strapped them above my skates, they would cover everything from my shins to my knee cap. The pads were about an inch thick, stuffed with heaven-knows-what, but seemed to my eager mind to be the perfect substitute for the real thing.

So, there I was in the nets, *sans* regular pads, *sans* goalie stick, but secure in the knowledge that, at last, the crease was mine to defend.

And defend it I did; nobly and with vigor for about five minutes. At that point, a forward on the other team powered his way past our backcheckers and moved to a position about 15 feet from my kneecaps.

I tensed, as only Turk Broda would have tensed, awaiting the drive.

I had a clear view of the shot. The black biscuit orbited from his stick and moved speedily yet vividly to my right. Confidently, I sized up my move with the insight of a centerfielder who knows precisely when to make his leap to haul down the long drive.

My right leg flashed out to deflect my enemy's shot into the corner. The timing couldn't have been more exquisite if I was using radar.

The save was brilliant, if I do say so myself, and with it went my brief goaltending career.

I had made one meaningful mistake. I had neglected to check the pads to be sure they had still been wound around the side of my kneecaps. Alas! The adhesive tape had come loose and the pads were just flat, leaving the sides of my knee completely vulnerable.

The puck squarely struck the inside of my right knee at a point where some nameless nerve exists. I watched in indescribable pain as the puck skimmed to my defenseman, who swung around and skated away from yours truly.

Within seconds, the initial pain subsided and I realized that I had to become vertical again if I wanted to blunt the next attack.

As play swirled around the opposite goal, I pressed firmly on my right skate in an attempt to regain my position.

To my horror and amazement, nothing happened. Absolutely nothing! I can't explain in medical terms what the puck did to my knee nerve, but I can assure you that ten shots of Novocain would not have rendered it any more inert.

By this time our attack had fizzled and the opposition was hustling back in my direction. I pressed once, twice, three times and couldn't budge.

"Get up!" my teammate Jimmy Hernon shouted.

"I CAN'T!" I yelled back. "My leg won't move."

Mercifully, the enemy skater understood my vulnerability and held up on his shot just as he reached our defensive perimeter.

The game was briefly halted and I was hauled to a snowbank

where I wondered whether I ever would stand on my own two feet again.

Within ten minutes, a semblance of feeling returned to my wounded joint and a half-hour later, I actually was able to approximate skating.

"Are you going back in goal?" Jimmy Hernon wondered.

"No," I replied, "I don't think so, not for the rest of my life!"

From that moment on, I appreciated goaltending from the safer distance, but studied the art form as much as I ever had, if not more intensely.

My favorite goalies were an odd mixture of rubberstoppers, but I leaned toward oddballs.

My first idol was a chap named Muzz Muvvoy who played for the U.S. Coast Guard team during World War II. The Cutters, as they were known, were part of the Eastern League and regularly appeared at Madison Square Garden. Murray's finely chiseled face appealed to me along with his style. Only later did I learn that he had been a minor league star in the Midwest U.S.

After the war, I took a liking to Nick Pidsodny, a combative netminder who thought nothing of skating far out of his net to challenge his foe. Pidsodny — a wonderfully-sounding name — played for the Baltimore Blades, also in the Eastern League.

Being an avid Toronto Maple Leafs fan, I, of course, adored Turk Broda and then his angular successor, Al Rollins. The latter epitomized the classically elegant, tall stand-up goalie who specialized in spectacular kick saves. Rollins shared a Vezina Trophy with Broda in 1950-51 when Toronto won its fourth Stanley Cup in five years. He later won a Hart Trophy for a last place Chicago Blackhawks squad, which told me a lot about Rollins' ability.

I later became enamored of Glenn Hall's work, particularly after he left Detroit for Chicago. As a Blackhawk, Mister Goalie developed the "V" formation (dropping to his knees with the legs fanning out in an inverted "V") which now is euphemistically called The Butterfly.

No goalie has ever matched Hall for durability and artistry combined. He played more than 500 consecutive games without a mask at the very highest level, and that's why Hall is rated tops in my book.

Speaking of masks, I was a witness at Madison Square Garden on November 2, 1959 when the Rangers' Andy Bathgate fired a sizzling drive that struck a maskless Jacques Plante directly in the face. The Canadiens goaltender dropped to the ice in a pool of blood and remained in what appeared to be desperate condition for several minutes. Eventually, he was helped to Madison Square Garden infirmary where repairs were made.

Nobody in the crowd was quite sure what the Canadiens would do, since they didn't carry a spare netminder in those days. After an interminably long delay, a figure wearing a Canadiens jersey strode down the corridor, up five steps and out onto the ice.

It was Jacques Plante, all right, but his face was covered with a grotesque mask with huge holes around the eyes and a painted covering over the nose. At the sight of Plante, the audience seemed to get a collective case of lockjaw. After all, they had never seen anything like this before.

Meanwhile, Plante moved between the pipes, took about a dozen warmup shots and then pronounced himself fit to continue. Naturally, everyone wondered how he would perform with his strange face-covering. The answer was quickly affirmative. Jacques was as synchronized and as sharp as ever and handily beat the Rangers that night.

Whether he could "beat" his coach, Toe Blake, was another story. After the game, we journalists congregated around Blake for his observations. All of us knew that Toe was the ultimate macho coach and the mask instinctively turned him off. Blake made it clear that he expected Plante to eschew the mask, post-haste, and return to the goal in his natural full-face form.

But Jacques' belief in the mask was as firm as his coach's conviction it was folly. In a rare show of defiance for that era, Plante refused to play unless he was allowed the mask. Blake grudgingly conceded, providing his goalie demonstrated that he could win. Plante responded with an impressive string of victories and the Canadiens won another Stanley Cup, this time with the masked goalie!

Plante's innovation won few followers at first. But as the slapshot's speed increased with lighter, curved-bladed sticks, prudent goaltenders gradually, and often grudgingly, tried the face-guard, and liked it.

The last of the maskless goalies were Lorne "Gump" Worsley of the Minnesota North Stars and Andy Brown who played for the World Hockey Association's Indianapolis Racers.

My obsession with goaltenders continued into the 1970s when Bill Smith emerged as a combative force for the New York Islanders. Although reviled by purists, Smith always seemed to me to be the ultimate crusader for goalie rights. "Battlin' Billy" implicitly believed in the sanctity of the crease and dealt out punishment to the interlopers.

I might add that Smith played the best single game I ever watched. This was the opener of the 1983 Islanders-Oilers series at Northlands Coliseum. Edmonton's attack formations, led by Wayne Gretzky, Mark Messier, Glenn Anderson and Jari Kurri, poured volley after volley at Smith and scored nothing. The Islanders won the match 2-0, and then swept the series in four games.

The second-best goaltending performance I had the pleasure to witness was Kelly Hrudey's four-time overtime masterpiece over Washington that ran from Easter Sunday eve through the early hours of Easter Sunday itself. Hrudey out-dueled Bob Mason in that classic.

From time to time, young hockey aficionados ask me to compare today's goaltenders with their predecessors from the 1940s, 1950s, 1960s and 1970s.

I immediately point out how drastically the game has changed in terms of skating speed, advanced weaponry and, of course, the much higher-velocity shots than ever before.

It's not that a Pavel Bure shoots the puck harder than a Bobby Hull once did, but rather that virtually everybody right down to the sixth defenseman is able to bomb drives at the net.

Whatever the case, goaltending remains one of the most challenging professions in all sports and goaltenders, in my estimation, are among the most laudable athletes I've ever had the pleasure to meet.

To provide you, the reader, with the broadest possible view of netminding, I have relied on personal observation and research as well as oral history.

The early days of goaltending are covered both in anecdotal form as well as personality profiles, some of which were adapted from my original McGraw-Hill Ryerson work, *Hockey's 100.*

Since nothing beats a first-person view of rubberstopping, I have included a wealth of interviews conducted with goalies past (Johnny Bower, Mike Palmateer, et al.) as well as innumerable contemporaries from 1994 NHL Rookie-of-the-Year Martin Brodeur to 1994 Vezina Trophy-winner Dominik Hasek. In some cases the tape recordings were edited into narrative form and, in others, the raw question-and-answer style was employed to create the aura of back-and-forth dialogue.

Our intention was to cover as broad a spectrum as possible. Thus, we dealt with the moderns — such diverse characters as French-Canadian Calder Trophy winner Martin Brodeur and Czech-born Dominik Hasek — in contrast with veteran aces like Kelly Hrudey and Chris Terreri.

Hopefully this book will reflect our admiration for goaltenders, a respect that was permanently etched in my mind the moment the puck caromed off the inside of my kneecap.

Stan Fischler, 1994

I

THE WAY IT WAS

THE PERSONALITIES

-1-
Georges Vezina

"The Vezina!" How often we have equated the name with the goaltending excellence. Since 1927, the Vezina Trophy has been awarded to the netminders who have delivered the lowest goals-against average each season.

More than any National Hockey League prize, this one has the deepest meaning, because Georges Vezina, after whom the trophy is named, was a *nonpareil* athlete whose ability was matched only by his infinite sportsmanship.

A gangling six-footer, Vezina guarded the Montreal Canadiens nets when the team played in the National Hockey Association, and later for the Habitants when the National Hockey League was organized.

In each milieu he excelled. The Canadiens won the NHA championship twice with Vezina between the pipes, and won three NHL championships and two Stanley Cups. He played a total of 373 consecutive games for Les Canadiens in an era when goaltenders' masks were unheard of. He was nicknamed "The Chicoutimi Cucumber" for his birthplace and his ability to remain cool under fire.

Vezina starred for the Canadiens for 15 years, from 1910 to 1925, and no doubt would have remained the master of his trade for several more seasons had he not been fatally stricken with tuberculosis. A quiet man, Vezina continued to play although he was aware that his life was doomed.

On November 28, 1925, his body wracked with pain, Vezina skated out onto the ice of Mount Royal Arena to face the visiting

Pittsburgh sextet. "No one knew," wrote author Ron McAllister, "that the great goaltender had struggled to the arena despite a temperature of 105 degrees.

"A deathlike chill settled over him, but with Pittsburgh forcing the play from the face-off, Vezina functioned throughout the first period with his usual dextrous ease, deflecting shot after shot. In the dressing room, he suffered a severe arterial hemorrhage, but the opening of the second period found him at his customary place in goal."

Fighting desperately against the fatigue and fever that completely throttled his body, the great Vezina could no longer see the puck as it skimmed from one side of the rink to the other. Suddenly, a collective gasp engulfed the arena. Vezina had collapsed in the goal crease. "In the stricken arena," said one observer, "all was silent as the limp form of the greatest of goalies was carried slowly from the ice."

It was the end of the trial for Georges and he knew it. At his request, he was taken home to his native Chicoutimi, where doctors diagnosed his case as advanced tuberculosis.

On March 24, 1926, he passed away. An enormous funeral, held in the old cathedral at Chicoutimi, saw players and fans from all parts of the country deliver their final tribute to the gallant goaltender. A year later, the Canadiens owners donated a trophy in his honor.

Georges Vezina was born in January 1887 in Chicoutimi, Quebec, a city that sits on the edge of the dark Saguenay River and flows into the blue St. Lawrence at historic Tadoussac.

Although young Vezina established himself as a class-A goalie even as a youth in Chicoutimi, he had developed a habit of playing without skates. For some peculiar reason, he found the idea of wearing skates a bother, and it wasn't until two years before he graduated to Les Canadiens that he actually learned to wear skates while tending goal.

Conceivably, the Montrealers might never have discovered Vezina were it not for a chance exhibition game between the Canadiens and the local Chicoutimi club on February 23, 1910. The match between the awesome professionals from Montreal and the patchwork amateur outfit figured to be so one-sided that only a handful of fans turned out for it.

Chicoutimi hardly looked like a formidable foe, except for the six-foot goalie wearing a red-and-white Habitant toque. Leaning against the goal post, the tall, lanky Vezina appeared to be too bored for words. But once the overpowering Canadiens sliced through the fragile Chicoutimi defense, Vezina suddenly responded with a peripatetic style that thoroughly dumbfounded the pros. Try as they might, the Canadiens could not score. Chicoutimi won the game, 2-0.

That was all the Canadiens' high command had to know. They invited Vezina to Montreal and he made his debut on December 31, 1910. Curiously, Georges never signed a contract with the Montrealers; he preferred a gentleman's handshake with his managers, first Joe Cattarinich and later Leo Dandurand.

The father of 22 children, Vezina was virtually impregnable once he took his position in the goal crease. Once, during a game at Hamilton, Bert Corbeau smashed into him with such force that the goaltender's head was cut open and his nose broken. Vezina continued playing despite the wounds, his ability undiminished by pain.

According to hockey historians, Vezina was the author of several hockey classics, including the 1916 Stanley Cup final between Les Canadiens and the Pacific Coast Hockey Association's Portland Rosebuds. The best-of-five series went to the limit, the final game being played on March 30, 1916. With the score tied 1-1, Vezina defused the most explosive Portland offensives until Goldie Prodgers scored the winner for Montreal. Vezina and each of his Stanley Cup-winning teammates received $238 for taking the championship.

In the Roaring Twenties, Vezina was better than ever. During the 1923-24 season, he allowed only 48 goals in 24 games, including three shutouts for a 2.00 goals against average. He then blanked Ottawa, 1-0, in the NHL playoff opener and sparkled as Montreal swept the series. Montreal went on to rout Calgary and Vancouver for the Stanley Cup. Vezina's Stanley Cup record was six goals in six games — an even 1.00 average.

By this time, Vezina's body was afflicted with the early symptoms of tuberculosis. "Beads of perspiration formed on his forehead for no apparent reason," said Ron McAllister. "An expression of pain flitted momentarily across his face, but the Great Vezina invariably settled down to the business at hand, turning in his usual matchless performance."

During the 1924-25 season, despite the ailment, he came up with a 1.90 goals-against average, easily the best in the league. But when he arrived at the Canadiens training camp in the fall of 1925, he seemed unusually fatigued.

It has been said that not even those in his own family realized that Vezina was fighting for his life as he prepared for the 1925-26 season. This would be a particularly fascinating year for the worldly Vezina. The NHL was expanding into the United States more than ever. It had embraced a Boston franchise a year earlier, and now New York and Pittsburgh had been added, as well as a second Montreal team, the Maroons, who would provide an English-speaking team as natural rivals for the Canadiens. Needless to say, the outstanding attraction in the American cities among the Montreal players was the redoubtable Vezina.

Sadly, "The Chicoutimi Cucumber" donned the *bleu, blanc, et rouge* uniform for the last time in the season opener of the 1925-26 season. There were 6,000 spectators in the stands on that rainy night who had come to see the great Vezina.

Few realized as he left the ice after a scoreless first period that he was bleeding from the mouth. But they began to perceive his pain in the second period when he fell to the ice for the last time.

Georges Vezina was the personification of courage and capability. When someone in hockey says "The Vezina," they need say no more.

-2-
Charlie Gardiner

Only his relatively brief career prevented Charlie "Chuck" Gardiner from receiving a higher place among the all-time goaltenders. Certainly, there have been few better during any of the game's epochs.

Before illness cut short his career, Gardiner played seven years with the Chicago Blackhawks, produced 42 shutouts, and had a remarkable 2.13 goals-against average. He won the Vezina Trophy (best goalie) in 1932 and repeated it in 1934. Thrice (1931, 1932, 1934) he was voted to the First All-Star Team and in 1933 made the Second Team.

The Blackhawks had never won a Stanley Cup championship until 1934, and it was then, thanks to Gardiner's efforts, that they prevailed. He permitted only 12 goals in eight playoff games for a 1.50 average.

Gardiner was one of the first of a legion of Windy City hockey heroes and Chuck, few could dispute, helped plant the seed of hockey interest in that city. A cocky Scotsman, he nevertheless distracted fans from an abysmally weak Blackhawks team.

Charles Robert Gardiner was born on December 31, 1904 in Edinburgh, Scotland, and arrived in Canada with his family in 1911. He grew up in hockey-mad Winnipeg during the 1920s and was discovered in 1925 while playing for a team in Selkirk, Manitoba.

Signed by the Winnipeg Maroons, he played through the 1926-27 season unaware that the Blackhawks were scouting him. He was signed by Chicago owner Major Frederic McLaughlin and played poorly in his first four game with the Blackhawks. Shortly thereafter he turned it around and was en route to permanent stardom.

One could fill a volume detailing Gardiner's exploits. A game against the powerful Boston Bruins is a case in point. Eddie Shore, the premier defenseman of the Bruins, was zooming in on Gardiner for a shot when the Blackhawk goalie edged out of his crease to meet him. In this way, Gardiner trimmed down the shooter's angle and forced Shore to shoot wide of the target. Undaunted, Shore pursued the puck behind the net, but Gardiner wheeled around and tripped the big Bruin.

In those days, the NHL awarded one-minute penalties to goalies, and Gardiner was ordered off the ice. While he sat out his foul, teammate Wentworth moved into the nets without the benefit of goaltender's equipment and managed to blunt the Bruins' attack.

Meanwhile, the impatient Gardiner was leaning on the boards awaiting the moment when he would finally spring from the penalty box. When his sentence expired, he leaped over the wooden boards and dashed headlong for the goal.

At the moment Gardiner was released, Boston defenseman George Owen captured the puck. He carefully aimed for the four-by-six-foot opening and drilled the rubber for what appeared to be a goal. But it never went in. Charlie had made the save.

By 1929, Gardiner had improved so much that he finished second to the immortal George Hainsworth of the Montreal Canadiens in the race for the Vezina Trophy. In 1932, he would finally win the coveted prize and be named to the All-Star Team. Charlie was the one piece of pure gold on the roster, and the lever that could catapult the Hawks to the heights of greatness.

In 1932-33, the Blackhawks finished fourth — out of the playoffs. The following year, they rallied and launched their most serious assault on first place. That they failed by seven points and finished second to Detroit was no fault of Gardiner's. His goaltending reached new degrees of perfection. He allowed only 83 goals in 48 games and registered 10 shutouts. In 14 other games, he permitted just one goal.

But astute Gardiner watchers perceived that there was something unusual about the goalie's deportment, and they couldn't figure out just what it was. Gardiner had lost his jovial manner and appeared to be melancholy.

Unknown to everyone, Gardiner was suffering from a chronic tonsil infection. The disease had spread and had begun to cause uremic convulsions. However, the goaltender pressed on. Winning the Stanley Cup became an obsession with him, and the Blackhawks responded by defeating first the Canadiens and then the Montreal Maroons. This put them in the Cup finals against the awesome Detroit Red Wings.

The best-of-five series opened in Detroit and the Blackhawks won the first game, 2-1, in double overtime. In the second, also at Detroit's Olympia Stadium, the Hawks ran away with the game, 4-1. When the teams returned to Chicago for the third, and what appeared to be the final game, all hands were ready to concede the Stanley Cup to the Blackhawks.

But it was not to be Charlie Gardiner's night. His body was wracked with pain, and he prayed that he might recapture his physical condition of seasons past. Charlie moved between the pipes for two periods, but the relentless Detroit attack overcame him in the third. Detroit won the game, 5-2.

Gardiner collapsed on a bench in the dressing room minutes after the final buzzer, but recovered quickly enough to realize that, psychologically, the Blackhawks were collapsing with him. Summoning all the strength at his command, Charlie peered across the room and said: "Look, all I want is one goal next game. Just one goal and I'll take care of the other guys."

On April 10, 1934 Gardiner returned to the crease, hunched his shoulders, tapped his pads, and prepared for battle. His body was numb from fatigue, but he was determined to overcome the pain and play his game.

For two periods, Gardiner had never been better. He held the Detroiters scoreless, but the Blackhawks were also unable to score. Even as it drained him of energy, Gardiner screamed encouragement to his players, but it was to no avail. The red-shirted Detroiters' counterattack developed new intensity, and Charlie did all he could to keep them at bay. He did, and the game went into sudden-death overtime.

There were those who doubted that Gardiner could sustain both the physical and mental strain much longer, yet when the overtime began he was smiling and even waved his stick to the crowd. For another 20 minutes, he blunted the best shots the enemy could hurl at him, but his teammates could do no better, and a second sudden-death period was required.

Charlie could no longer smile. Flames of pain burned his insides as he tried to concentrate on the black rubber disk. The overtime had begun again, and for ten minutes there was no resolution. Suddenly, little Mush March of the Blackhawks took command, skating into Detroit ice. He cracked his wrist and the puck took off and sailed past Wilf Cude and into the net. The time was 10:05 when the Blackhawks had annexed their first Stanley Cup.

Gardiner hurled his stick in the air and then just barely made it back to the dressing room under the backslaps of his teammates.

The roar of the crowd had hardly subsided when Charlie was taken to the hospital. He underwent brain surgery, and following the operation died on June 13, 1934.

Those who watched Gardiner in action on a regular basis suggest that he was the greatest of all time. Certainly, in seven years of NHL play he demonstrated an uncanny puckstopping ability. However, his career was too short to permit inclusion on a higher plane, although this in no way diminishes Gardiner's accomplishments.

-3-

Roy Worters

The dream of every hockey scout in search of a goaltender is to find a man who is agile, but also tall and wide so that he can fill as much of the six-feet-wide by four-feet-high entrance to the net as possible. Some of the greatest netminders, from Georges Vezina to Ken Dryden, were big men who filled much of the air space leading to the net. All of which helps explain why Roy Worters was such a marvel at his profession.

Worters was a goalie who measured only 5'3" and 130 pounds, yet his stature, compared to other notables who guarded the twine, remains immense to this day. And the fact that he generally played for inferior clubs, such as the New York Americans, merely adds to his glitter.

His drawbacks notwithstanding, Roy was the Hart Trophy winner in 1929 as the National Hockey League's most valuable player, the Vezina Trophy (best goalie) winner in 1931, and was twice voted to the Second All-Star Team (1932 and 1934).

Worters is best remembered for his heroic performances with the Americans, but he actually broke into the majors as a member of the Pittsburgh Pirates, which joined the NHL in the fall of 1925. After a salary dispute with the Pirates, Worters was traded to the Amerks for the then-unheard-of sum of $25,000 plus two players.

The deal was the bane of Worters' hockey life at first. Hard-nosed galleryites at Madison Square Garden taunted him with catcalls. "So, you're worth twenty-five grand, eh? Worters, you're not worth twenty-five cents!" At first, the goalie who, inevitably, had become known as "Shrimp," was distressed by the insults, but gradually he pulled his game together and captured the imagination of Madison Square Garden spectators. After one match he received a standing ovation. Shortly thereafter, Worters had the distinction of losing a game to the Montreal Canadiens without a goal being scored against him. It was a 0-0 tie late in the match when Howie Morenz of the Canadiens broke into the clear for a shot at Worters. Roy stopped the blistering drive, deflecting it into the corner. But as Morenz unleashed his shot, "Bullet" Joe Simpson of the Americans tossed his stick at Morenz. In those days, the stick-throwing foul was punishable with an automatic goal. Montreal won the game, 1-0.

"Although Roy never saw the Stanley Cup awarded to his team," said Ron McAllister, "he won every individual honor that a goalkeeper could possibly earn, and more. The thought of what he might have achieved with a winning team before him makes him a man of mystery in the record books."

Worters could have gained entrance to the Hockey Hall of Fame purely on guts. He suffered 216 stitches in his face alone, and continued playing despite the pain of cracked ribs, a broken kneecap, three broken toes, and countless lesser injuries, including the loss of eight teeth.

Roy Worters was born October 19, 1900, in Toronto, the son of a trolley car motorman. When he was old enough to carry a load, Roy began delivering milk for his uncle's dairy. In return, Roy received free milk. "The future goalkeeper knew the lesson of work before he learned the meaning of life," said a friend.

He began his hockey career as a forward and remained up front until he was 17 when the goal-weak Toronto Riverdales searched for someone to tend the twine. Roy volunteered, and the Riverdales suddenly began winning games. Eventually, he moved up the Junior ranks to the Toronto Canoe Club.

The Canoe Club, with Worters performing uncanny feats in goal, marched to the Memorial Cup, symbol of Junior hockey supremacy in Canada. One of Roy's most formidable opponents was a young wiz named Howie Morenz, who later would ripen as a superstar with the Montreal Canadiens. "Morenz," Worters once said, "is some wild wind, that number 7 of the Canadiens. To me, he's just a blur — 77777!"

To Morenz, Worters was like a wall in front of the upright, despite his minuscule size. Over a span of 488 games, Worters' goals-allowed average was 2.36 — uncanny considering the feeble defense in front of him.

Worters also was an innovator. He was the first netminder to direct rebounds into the corners of the rink with the back of his gloves and, needless to say, demonstrated that a Lilliputian goalie could be as good as a big man with the pads.

At the age of 37, he was still blocking shots for the Amerks when he suffered a severe hernia and was hospitalized. Red Dutton, who had become manager of the team, believed that Roy was capable of a comeback and offered Worters a sizable sum to return to the wars, but the goalie declined and returned to his native Toronto.

"When Roy quit the game," said Ron McAllister, "few players or fans remained untouched by his tremendous contribution to the game."

A foe who had been frustrated by Worters for several seasons, said later: "For years after Roy left the game it was hard to realize that he had been gone from the NHL for good."

He stayed close to the sport he loved so well and worked with the NHL Oldtimers Association, as well as local charities. He was inducted into the Hockey Hall of Fame in 1969, twelve years after he died of throat cancer. He was a David among Goliaths.

-4-

Turk Broda

"The Turk" was fat and funny. And perhaps that is the reason why he was often bypassed when the cream of the goalkeeping fraternity was discussed.

Had he been a tragic figure like Terry Sawchuk, a worrier like Glenn Hall, or an eccentric like Jacques Plante, Broda might receive more serious consideration, but the image of Toronto's fabulous fat man always was light and upbeat — except when it came to the big games.

While he is fondly remembered for winning his "Battle of the Bulge" campaign against excess poundage, Broda is also revered by historians for his impeccable ability to excel in the most critical moments.

Therefore, it is not surprising that he twice won the Vezina Trophy for having the best goals against average, was twice a First Team All-Star, once a Second Team All-Star, and played for five Stanley Cup-winning teams.

Broda, along with center Syl Apps, formed the cornerstone of manager Conn Smythe's rebuilding effort when Toronto began its ascent to dizzying heights in the 1940s. The Cup win in 1942 was the first for Broda. Following service in World War II, he returned to help Toronto win an unprecedented three consecutive Cups (1947, 1948, 1949) and still another in 1951.

Turk had the ideal disposition for a goaltender and was a superb team player on a club sprinkled with scintillating characters.

It could be said that Bill Durnan, who starred in goal for Montreal during the same era, was a better textbook goalie than Broda and produced superior averages, but Durnan couldn't match the Turk, neither in Stanley Cups nor longevity. Broda became a big-leaguer before Durnan arrived, and outlasted him by two seasons.

The records indicate that Broda's best season — statistically speaking — was 1940-41, when he rang up a 2.06 goals-against average. But the vintage Broda appeared during the 1942 playoffs when he starred in the seventh (Cup-winning) game of the finals and in 1947-48 when he powered the Leafs to a first-place finish, won the Vezina, and then, surrounded by one of the most formidable teams in history, annexed the Stanley Cup.

Yet, many Torontonians prefer the memory of November 1949 when Smythe demanded that a number of his stars trim their waistline in a hurry. The anti-fat edict made headlines throughout North America.

Although Smythe singled out defenseman Garth Boesch and forwards Howie Meeker, Harry Watson, Vic Lynn and Sid Smith for his blasts, the key target of Smythe's ire was his longtime goaltending stalwart, Broda.

Smythe's opening gun in the "Battle of the Bulge" was a demand that his players reduce their weight to specified limits. Broda, who weighed 197 pounds, was ordered to lose seven pounds. To underline the seriousness of his offensive, Smythe promptly called up reserve goalie Gil Mayer from his Pittsburgh farm team. It was Tuesday and he was giving Turk until Saturday to fulfill the demand. "I'm taking Broda out of the nets," Smythe said, "and he's not going back until he shows some common sense."

Smythe's outburst reverberated across Canada and parts of the United States, and soon "The Battle of the Bulge" became a *cause célèbre*. Neutral observers regarded Turk's tussle with the scales as a huge joke, win or lose, but to the Toronto boss it was no joke. None of the Leafs were particularly amused, either.

After one day of severe dieting, Turk trimmed his weight from 197 to 193 pounds, and all of Canada seemed to breathe easier. Smythe had set the final weigh-in for Saturday afternoon, just before the evening match against the New York Rangers at Maple Leaf Gardens. He refused to divulge what specific action he would take against Broda or the other Leafs if they did not measure up, but he suggested that it would not be lenient. Turk moved forward and gingerly placed his feet on the platform. The numbers finally settled — just under 190 pounds. He had made it! Turk was delighted, and Smythe was doubly enthusiastic, because he regarded his goaltender with paternal affection. "There may be better goalies around somewhere," said the manager, "but there's no greater sportsman than the Turkey. If the Rangers score on him tonight, I should walk out and hand him a malted milk, just to show I'm not trying to starve him to death."

That night, Maple Leaf Gardens was packed with 13,359 Turk fans, and when Broda skated out for the opening face-off, the

Gardens' regimental band swung into "Happy Days Are Here Again" and followed with a chorus of "She's Too Fat for Me."

Referee George Gravel dropped the puck to start the game, and the Rangers immediately swarmed in on Broda. This time, however, he was the Turk of old.

Broda's slimmer teammates couldn't beat goalie Chuck Rayner of the Rangers, however, and the first period ended with the teams tied 0-0. It was the same story in the second period, as each team desperately probed for an opening. The Rangers got their big break late in the middle period when Pentti Lund found his opening hole and fired the puck mightily, but somehow Broda thrust his pad in the way and deflected the rubber out of danger. The fans rose and toasted Turk with a standing ovation, and when the second period ended, the contest remained a scoreless deadlock.

Early in the third period, the Leafs were attempting a change in the lines when Howie Meeker and Vic Lynn, two of the marked fat men, combined to feed a lead pass to Max Bentley, who normally wouldn't have been on the ice with them. Bentley moved through the Rangers checkers and unleashed a steaming shot that flew past Rayner. Later in the period another fat man, Harry Watson, skimmed a pass to Bill Ezinicki, who also beat Rayner.

Now all eyes were on the clock as it ticked toward the 20-minute mark and the end of the game. With only a minute remaining, Broda still had a shutout. The countdown began: ten, nine, eight, seven, six, five . . . the crowd was roaring as if the Leafs had won the Stanley Cup . . . four, three, two, one. The game was over; Turk dove for the puck and gathered it in. It was his symbolic trophy for winning the Battle of the Bulge.

Walter Broda was born May 15, 1914 in the wheat country of western Canada. His home town, Brandon, sent many a young hockey player to the professionals, but few appeared less likely to make it than the portly young netminder. Although his skating was poor and his reflexes lacked the spark of a thinner player, Broda earned a spot on the school team — by default. Luckily, his principal began working privately with his student, teaching him the finer points of goaltending until Broda's game began to improve. He soon caught on with a local club called the Brandon North Stars and played goal for them in a one-game playoff with the Elmwood Millionaires. Broda's club lost 11-1! In 1930-31, he somehow managed to take over the goalkeeping for the Manitoba Hydros, in the Brandon Commercial League. He played so capably in an intermediate league during that time that he was named to its All-Star team.

Broda got his break after trying out and failing his audition with the Brandon Native Sons, a top junior entry. Although the manager had rejected him, the Native Sons boss remembered Turk. He called Broda that spring when the regular Native Sons goaltender was ruled over-age in a last-minute discovery, and the junior club desperately needed a goaltender.

Amused rather than annoyed at the sudden turnabout by the Native Sons, Turk accepted their offer to take over the goaltending during the Memorial Cup playoffs for the Junior championship of Canada.

Brandon swept the series and Broda was at his best, as would always be the case, in the most excruciating moments. It was only a matter of time before he would make his way up to the ranks of the pros. Conn Smythe signed him in 1936 for what turned out to be one of the best moves ever made by one of hockey's most insightful entrepreneurs.

After his playing career, Broda took a number of coaching jobs in both amateur and professional ranks, the last of which was with Quebec in the American Hockey League. He died on October 17, 1972, much too soon, at the age of 58. The Turk will always be remembered as a happy performer, but most of all as a clutch champion.

-5-
Chuck Rayner

It is mind-boggling to imagine what dizzying heights Chuck Rayner might have reached if he had enjoyed the luxury of playing for a genuinely powerful hockey team. But such was not "Bonnie Prince Charlie's" good fortune. The bushy-browed goaltender made his debut with the New York (Brooklyn) Americans and finished his valorous puckblocking career with a rather pathetic New York Rangers aggregation.

In between, he demonstrated that he was either the very best, or certainly among the top three goalies in the world — despite the fact that he never had a first-place team or a Stanley Cup championship to show for it. Nevertheless, his hard-fought reputation spoke for itself.

Rayner made a permanent impression on the NHL and earned his way into the Hockey Hall of Fame. He is the only goaltender ever to have scored a goal by skating the length of the rink in an organized hockey game (although not in the NHL).

He was also among the very first to participate in what was then a revolutionary two-goalie experiment, along with his longtime sidekick and pal, James "Sugar Jim" Henry.

The 1949-50 season was in many ways the high point of Rayner's career, as he single-handedly led the Rangers to the Stanley Cup finals.

Playing for a mediocre Ranger team that never finished higher than fourth, Bonnie Prince Charlie led the Rangers to upset the Canadiens in the 1950 playoffs. They went on to the final round against the Detroit Red Wings. Playing not even one home game, they surprised the entire NHL with their strong bid, only to lose the seventh game in dramatic fashion — in an electrifying, double-overtime affair.

When he won the Hart Trophy in 1950, it was one of the most popular announcements in the annals of the game, as he was one of the nicest guys in the sport. Oddly enough, the year he won the Hart Trophy, he placed only fourth in the standings for the Vezina Trophy.

It was his remarkable and sensational performance in the 1950 playoffs that compensated for this. He was incredible during the series, making virtually impossible saves. Although the Rangers' quest for the Stanley Cup was stopped, the results of the voting for the Hart Trophy were a credit to the sportsmanship of hockey when the tall goaltender's name was announced.

He was only the second goaltender at that time to win the Hart Trophy. Rayner received 36 out of a possible 54 points for a 13-point lead over Ted Kennedy of the Toronto Maple Leafs. The great Maurice Richard of the Montreal Canadiens finished third in the balloting with 18 points.

Chuck made the Second Team All-Stars three times, in 1948-49, 1949-50 and 1950-51. In his eight seasons with the New York Rangers, encompassing 424 games, he had 24 shutouts, plus one shutout in the playoffs.

Rayner won the West Side Association Trophy as the Rangers' most valuable player during the years 1945-46 and 1946-47 and shared it in 1948-49 with Edgar Laprade.

In August 1973, Bonnie Prince Charlie was inducted into hockey's Hall of Fame in honor of his contributions to his sport.

Claude Earl Rayner was born in the small town of Sutherland, Saskatchewan, on August 11, 1920. Like all of the youngsters of that time and place, he went to the local skating rinks to play the national pastime. Chuck always wanted to be a goaltender. In 1936, when he was 16 years old, he was in goal when the Saskatoon Wesleys reached the Junior playoffs against the Winnipeg Monarchs. He then went into goal for the Kenora Thistles in 1936.

At the end of the 1939-40 season, Chuck went down to the New York Americans farm club, the Springfield Indians. Rayner had only played seven games for the Indians when Earl Robertson of the Americans suffered a head injury, leaving open a berth in the nets.

Rayner was called up to take over Robertson's place and so, in 1940, the young man from Sutherland was playing in the NHL.

Rayner played goal for the Americans throughout the 1941-42 season. He then went home and joined the Royal Canadian Armed Forces. Discharged from the service in 1945, Chuck returned to hockey to discover that the New York Americans had disbanded, and that all members of the team were to be part of a raffle for the other NHL teams.

Chuck Rayner's name was pulled out by Lester Patrick of the New York Rangers. And thus began one of the oddest stories in sports. Lester Patrick had already hired a goalie, Sugar Jim Henry. But Chuck finally won the goalkeeping job permanently.

Rayner had to retire after the 1952-53 season. He had damaged the cartilage in his knee. An operation temporarily held the knee up, but again, the knee weakened to the point where he felt he couldn't do the job anymore.

Chuck suffered through many injuries, and there's no telling how long he could have played if he had had a mask and an alternate goalkeeper.

After his retirement as a player, Rayner returned to western Canada where he coached the Nelson Leafs. After two years, he went to Alberta and coached the Edmonton Flyers. He then did some work for the Rangers, and then for the Detroit Red Wings organization with his friend Sid Abel.

By the mid-'60s, he had been coaching nine years, but didn't enjoy it. Chuck didn't like having to tell a kid that he was traded.

Chuck was a courageous man who was often black-and-blue. He was the kind of man who played when a lesser one would have sat out. It was tragic that such a nice guy with his capabilities never played on a Stanley Cup championship winner. However, no one will ever forget the heroics Rayner accomplished during the exciting 1950 playoffs with the Cinderella Rangers.

-6-

Terry Sawchuk

It was February 1, 1970, at Madison Square Garden in New York City and the Rangers were playing the Pittsburgh Penguins. In a losing cause on January 28 to the Kings at Los Angeles (in a hotly disputed game in which the Kings apparently scored a tie-breaking goal at the same second the game ended), coach Emile Francis had benched his first-string goaltender, Ed Giacomin, and replaced him with 20-year-veteran Terry Sawchuk.

Now the tired and out-of-shape netminder would be facing his second straight battle. Once the premier goaltender in the National Hockey League, Sawchuk was long past his prime and was making only his fourth start for New York in the whole season. Not many people in the Garden that night thought he could help the Rangers win.

But they were wrong. Not only did the Rangers win, but Sawchuk blanked the Penguins 6-0, notching the 103rd shutout of his long career. The record-setting whitewash occurred precisely 20 years and two weeks after he had been called up to the Detroit Red Wings from Indianapolis in the American Hockey League. In that game, he had posted his first NHL victory and his first shutout, 1-0, against the New York Rangers. No one else in NHL history had ever recorded 100 shutouts. The closest to Sawchuk in that department was the legendary George Hainsworth, with 94.

"That's the story of his career," said coach Francis after watching Sawchuk frustrate Pittsburgh, "not letting the puck get past him."

But not the whole story. The whole story of Terry Sawchuk was much, much more complicated than the triumph of 435 victories, 103 shutouts, four Vezina Trophies (1952, 1953, 1955 and one shared with Johnny Bower in 1965), four Stanley Cup rings (1952, 1954 and 1955 with Detroit; 1967 with Toronto) and the Calder Trophy as Rookie of the Year in 1951 (after winning Rookie of the Year honors in the USHL at age 18 and the AHL at 19). The whole story is darker and sadder than that.

The man who recorded his last shutout on February 1, 1970 had withered from a happy, chubby rookie to a chronic loner who had amassed 400 stitches in his face alone (before donning a goalie mask in 1964); was suffering acute depression because his wife had divorced him, and she retained custody of their seven children; and had such a long history of illness and injury that teammates sometimes referred to him as Mr. Blue Cross. More tragic yet, Terry Sawchuk, on that February night in 1970, was only three months away from his death, caused by a pulmonary embolism following a mysterious injury and three emergency surgeries.

"When I first met Terry, he was just a big, happy puppy dog," recalls Max McNab, the executive vice-president of the New Jersey Devils who roomed with Sawchuk during his rookie year with the Omaha Knights of the USHL in 1946-47. "He was probably the best goalie I ever saw, and certainly the biggest sleeper — that's all he did back at the boarding house!"

Sawchuk may have been a "happy puppy" back then, but his life had already been molded by tragedy. The Winnipeg, Manitoba native they called "Butch" started playing hockey as a defenseman in the city's East Kildonan section, but switched to goaltending at age ten. At about that same time, Sawchuk's older brother died, unbelievably, of a heart attack.

Less than two years later, he injured his arm while playing football. For months he walked around with a severely broken arm. When surgery was finally performed, Sawchuk's right arm remained permanently bent and two inches shorter than the left. Over the years, doctors removed more than 60 bone chips from the arm, giving him no further mobility, but relieving some of the chronic pain.

The litany of Sawchuk's sorrow and injuries seemed almost endless: in 1948 his right eyeball was slashed by a stick and required three stiches — on the eyeball. Then his appendix burst one season, followed soon after by a car crash which left him with a collapsed lung and more surgery. Once, when he was suffering from badly pinched nerves, he was kept in a hospital bed and only allowed out to play hockey games!

Interspersed with the bitter was the sweet. In 1952, when Detroit swept the Stanley Cup in eight playoff games, Terry had four shutouts and gave up a meager 0.62 goals per game. From 1950-51 through 1954-55, his goals-against average was less than 2.00 and he compiled 56 shutouts in those same few seasons.

Then, in 1955, at the peak of Sawchuk's young career, after the Red Wings had won their second Cup in a row and their third in four years, Detroit GM Jack Adams decided to trade him. Sawchuk went to Boston with Vic Stasiuk, Marcel Bonin and Lorne Davis for Ed Sandford, Real Chevrefils, Norm Corcoran, Gilles Boisvert and Warren Godfrey.

This would be a turning point for Sawchuk, in more ways than one. Even though he still earned nine shutouts in 1955-56, his average climbed to 2.36, he led the league in losses with 33, and more significantly, he had the league high in penalty minutes for a goalie, with 20. The surliness and lack of cooperation with the press that would become infamous throughout the league began in earnest during his stay in Boston. And his weight plummeted, from more than 200 pounds to less than 180. For the rest of his life, Sawchuk would be trying to gain weight instead of shedding it.

In the midst of the 1956-57 season, Sawchuk walked out on the Bruins. It turned out that he was suffering from the first — and, until 1970, the worst — of several bouts of depression, as well as a hefty case of mononucleosis. When asked how it felt to have the acute virus, Sawchuk, in what was then a rare response to the press, said, "It feels like the white corpuscles and the red corpuscles have taken sides and are fighting each other in my veins."

Sawchuk was traded back to the Red Wings in 1957 and played the entire schedule for the club, but he wasn't the same goalie. His average that season climbed to 2.96 and again led the league in penalty minutes for goalies with 39. The man known for having the reflexes of a snake and a unique style of bending over from the waist in order to see through the bodies in front of him, appeared to be losing it.

Finally, in 1964, Sawchuk was left unprotected by Detroit in the waiver draft and Toronto picked him up for a minuscule $20,000 draft price. Two years after coming to Toronto, it was dicovered that Sawchuk had two ruptured disks in his lower spine. After fusion surgery, Sawchuk's play improved considerably, culminating in his finest performance on April 15, 1967 — at the age of 37 — in the fifth game of the Stanley Cup semi-finals between the Leafs and the Chicago Blackhawks. Goaltending partner Johnny Bower was having a shaky game and was pulled in the second period. The game was tied, 2-2, as was the best-of-seven series at two apiece.

In came Sawchuk and within two minutes The Golden Jet, Bobby Hull, streaked to within 15 feet of Sawchuk's left and from an almost impossible angle parallel to the goal mouth, let loose a bullet which hit Sawchuk on the left shoulder and literally knocked him down.

Bob Haggert, the Maple Leafs trainer, ran across the ice to Sawchuk: "Where'd you get it?"

Said Sawchuk from his knees, "On my bad shoulder."

"Think you're all right?" asked Haggert.

"I stopped the damn puck, didn't I?" came the usual terse and slightly defiant Sawchuk response.

Toronto went on to win the game and the Cup, but then they rewarded Sawchuk by leaving him unprotected in the 1967 expansion draft, and he was picked up by the new Los Angeles Kings. Unfortunately, the Kings had chosen Sawchuk not because they thought he could still win games in the nets, but because he had a famous hockey name, and famous names were worth a lot in Los Angeles.

But they had chosen the wrong man to wield a positive public image for the new team. As usual, Sawchuk's treatment of both the media and the fans ranged from surly to stonily mute. After a year in California, the Kings traded Sawchuk back to Detroit. After appearing in only 13 games during the 1968-69 season with the Red Wings, Sawchuk was traded to the Rangers with Sandy Snow for Larry Jeffrey.

Sawchuk would see action in only eight more NHL games, including the shutout of Pittsburgh in which he showed flashes of the form that had made him the league's best goaltender.

Ten weeks later, the season was over. Sawchuk had just returned to the New York area from a failed attempt to reconcile with his wife when he got into a squabble with teammate and roommate Ron Stewart at the E&J Pub on Long Island. The fight was over $184 that Stewart claimed he had paid on their shared apartment, arguing that Sawchuk owed him half of that amount. The two were separated in the bar but resumed the fight outside.

Finally they disappeared, only to be found later on the lawn in front of their apartment building. The two had started up again (later reports and Sawchuk's subsequent admission made it fairly clear that it was Sawchuk who started the physical part of the quarrel each time), but this time Sawchuk had fallen on Stewart, and as he did so his midsection struck either Stewart's knee or a small portable barbecue which had fallen over in the fracas.

However it happened, the result was that Terry Sawchuk suffered internal injuries that would prove to be fatal.

It would take three operations and a month before he would succumb to the same affliction that killed his brother 30 years earlier — a heart attack.

-7-

Jacques Plante

That Jacques Plante was the third-best goalie of all time is an assertion that few could challenge. That Plante was the best goalie ever is a statement that could be supported in some quarters, although not this one. However, Plante's enormity in his field is certainly without question. He may not have been the iron man that Glenn Hall was with the Chicago Blackhawks nor the implacably perfect puckstopper that Georges Vezina had been during an earlier era with the Montreal Canadiens, but Plante was stupendous in his own right.

He was a winner. He was an expert. He was creative and he was durable. He won the Hart Trophy as the National Hockey League's most valuable player in 1962 and won the Vezina Trophy as the top goalie from 1956 through 1960 and again in 1962 and finally, sharing it with Glenn Hall, in 1969. He was named to the First All-Star Team in 1956, 1959 and 1962, and to the Second Team in 1957, 1958, 1960 and 1971.

Unlike Terry Sawchuk, whose skills eroded with time, Plante was in mint condition at the age of 40 when he starred for the St. Louis Blues. Plante played for six Stanley Cup-winning teams and eight clubs that finished in first place. And, more than Sawchuk, Plante was the most innovative of the modern goaltenders. In fact, it would be safe to say that Jacques did more to revolutionize the *modus operandi* of puckstopping than anyone in the past 30 years. On top of that, Plante, plainly and simply, was a very interesting character.

In his spare time, Plante, alias "Jake the Snake," had a hobby of knitting toques, the French-Canadian wool caps worn by his ancestors. He was confident and cocky, and betrayed a bizarre goaltending style that would soon be copied by other netminders around the league. It was Plante's idea that he would be aiding his defensemen by roaming out of his cage, formerly a strict taboo, and behind the net when the pucks were caromed off the boards and skidded in behind his cage. By doing so, Plante was able to control the puck and pass it off to a teammate, while scrambling back to his goal crease before any shots were taken. This style was introduced when the Canadiens, coached by Dick Irvin, were engaged in a thrilling semi-final against the Chicago Blackhawks in 1953.

All this was well and good and terribly fascinating, but for the adventurous and unconventional Plante to experiment with the Canadiens in the playoffs and on the brink of elimination was something else! But Irvin had made a commitment and Plante was his goalie. Jacques the Roamer immediately went into the cage and stopped the Blackhawks cold. He foiled a breakaway early in the fifth game, and with that impetus Les Canadiens won two straight games and captured the first round. Plante won himself a job and helped the Canadiens to the Stanley Cup. By the late 1950s, Montreal had the most formidable club of the decade — if not all time — with the defense of Doug Harvey and Tom Johnson complementing the enigmatic goalkeeper.

Still the best in the league, Jake the Snake occasionally enraged spectators with his scrambles behind the net for the puck. Once, the play backfired on him. He missed the disk; an opponent retrieved it and shoved the rubber into the yawning cage before Plante could return to guard it. In November 1958, Plante's goals-against average began climbing, matched by coach Toe Blake's temper.

The Blake-Plante repartee was, perhaps, even more ominous than it sounded. Severe to a fault, the coach was down on his goaltender and was to become more and more disenchanted with Plante's behavior as the season progressed.

It was ironic that the Plante-Blake rift widened at the precise point when Jacques executed one of his most courageous acts. The date was November 2, 1959. Plante was in the Canadiens net facing the Rangers at Madison Square Garden. Right wing Andy Bathgate of the Rangers, one of the league's hardest shooters, released a quick shot that struck Plante squarely on the nose and sent him bloodied to the ice. His face looking like a mashed potato laden with ketchup, Plante was helped to the dressing room where seven stitches were sewn into his pulverized proboscis.

Until then, Plante had been experimenting during practice sessions with a mask that was molded to his facial contours. Blake, an old-school hardliner, was irrevocably opposed to Jacques using the face piece in a regular game but, this time, the Canadiens had no spare goalie and Plante would not go back onto the ice without a mask. Blake had no choice but to oblige and, on that night, history was made. Plante wore the mask, won the game and vowed to continue wearing the device as long as he played. Blake was not the least enamored with the idea, although he publicly asserted that, as long as it helped Plante keep the pucks out of the net, it would be all right. For 1959-60, the mask proved effective enough to enable Plante to win the Vezina Trophy.

But Blake was a hard man and his grievances against Plante transcended the mask issue. The breaking point came in 1963 when he was dealt to the Rangers. Blake would have preferred it if Plante had displayed an uncompromising attitude toward the game; the kind that marked other Canadiens, mostly notably Maurice Richard. This, however, was not Plante's way. He pursued his unorthodoxy with the Rangers, then the St. Louis Blues, Toronto Maple Leafs and Boston Bruins.

Jacques Plante was born January 17, 1929, in Shawinigan Falls, Quebec, and like many a French-Canadian youngster, played his hockey on the outdoor rinks of La Belle Province. His goaltending excellence was unquestioned in the early 1950s, yet he was not given serious thought as a potential goalie for the Canadiens because they had a relatively young and efficient Gerry McNeil guarding the twines for them. But Dick Irvin took a dramatic gamble in 1953, and Plante rewarded him with a memorable clutch effort.

Plante concluded his NHL career with the Boston Bruins in April 1973, then became general manager-coach of the Quebec Nordiques in the World Hockey Association. It was another case of a superstar being unable to orchestrate from the sidelines as well as he had on the ice. A season later, at the age of 45, he returned to the nets, this time with the WHA's Edmonton Oilers. He played commendably for the Oilers, but finally retired for good at the conclusion of the campaign and became a part-time goaltending coach for the Philadelphia Flyers, a position he retained through the early 1980s. Plante died on February 27, 1986.

Through the years Plante rubbed several people the wrong way, and many have never forgotten what they interpreted as his abrasive manner. But no follower with a sense of hockey history will ever forget the comprehensive contributions made by Plante or his consummate skill at blocking a puck.

There was nobody like him before, and there will not be anyone like him again. An original. A craftsman.

-8-
Billy Smith

It is no coincidence that in the decade spanning 1975-85, the New York Islanders were one of the NHL's premier teams and that Bill Smith blossomed into one of the most memorable goaltenders on the continent. His renown is due to a distillation of artistry and durability and an unquenchable thirst for victory.

"In the 30 years I've played and coached pro hockey," said Don Cherry, now a commentator for *Hockey Night in Canada*, "there's never been a player who's wanted to win as bad as Smitty. That's why you won't find a better money goalie. And that goes for the great ones like Terry Sawchuk and Glenn Hall. And if you don't believe it, look at the record."

The arithmetic makes a better case for Smith's invincibility than attorneys F. Lee Bailey and Edward Bennett Williams ever could. Smith accumulated four Stanley Cup championship rings since his playoff debut in 1975, when he orchestrated the Islanders' arresting opening-round upset over the Rangers. Furthermore, "Bad Billy," as he was known to the foe, totaled 88 playoff wins (Terry Sawchuk had 54 and Glenn Hall had 49), won the Conn Smythe Trophy (playoff MVP, 1983), the Vezina Trophy (best goaltender, 1982), and the All-Star Game MVP Award (1982), shared the Jennings Trophy (best goals-against average, 1983) with then-teammate Roland Melanson, and had an All-Star berth (1982). "I'm a money goalie," he would say, with a combination of candor and simplicity that was his trademark.

No one could have guessed that there would be such accolades for the 5'10", 185-pound native of Perth, Ontario. Born December 12, 1950, Bill was the youngest son of Joe and Annie Smith, and since his older brothers had begun skating and playing long before he did, Billy became the family goaltender by default. "They were a lot better than I was," recalled Smith of his siblings. "That meant that they'd do the shooting and whether I liked it or not, I had to go in the net and stop them."

However, the youngster played well enough for the Cornwall Royals in 1969-70 to attract the attention of the NHL's Los Angeles

Kings. The Kings handed him a contract and dispatched Smith to Springfield of the American League. In two seasons, he totaled 55 penalty minutes, a figure that inspired Bill Torrey, who was putting the new Islanders franchise together, to scout the kid. Torrey was impressed, and drafted Smith in June 1972 for the original Islanders team. The rest is for the record books.

To those who viewed Smith in enemy rinks around the NHL, the husky son of Joe and Annie Smith was no less than Darth Vader on skates, a misanthrope who would think nothing of crippling Wayne Gretzky or removing Lindy Ruff's eye. Superficially, at least, this would appear to be the case if one peeks at Smith's scrapbook.

Bad Billy twice ignited international incidents by wreaking havoc with pretty-boy Gretzky. He feuded with such behemoths as Dave Semenko, Paul Holmgren and Terry O'Reilly, not to mention a smaller terror named Tiger Williams. Since turning pro in 1971, Smith often accumulated more penalties than some of his defensemen, and in 1978-79 he reached a career high of 54 penalty minutes.

Pinpointing the most egregious of Smith's transgression is a matter of endless debate among the Society for the Prevention of Cruelty to Crease-Crowders, but the assault on Lindy Ruff serves as an example of the divided views concerning the goalie's ethical standards. During the 1980 playoff between the Islanders and the Buffalo Sabres, several enemy forwards trespassed into Smith's inviolable crease — the area in front of the net that is technically off limits to enemy attackers. As is so often the case, the referee either did not see, or did not choose to see, the infractions committed in the four-by-eight-foot rectangle.

The Islanders goalie, however, took careful note of each incursion, and when Sabres rookie Lindy Ruff threatened to be yet another interloper during a match at Nassau Coliseum, it was only natural that Smith should raise his right arm, the one carrying the goalie stick, in the direction of his onrushing foe. The top of the stick shaft jolted Ruff in the eye, sending him to the ice contorted with pain. From the Sabres' viewpoint, it was an outrageous cheap shot, unprovoked and unnecessary — and although Ruff was not seriously hurt — grounds for severe punishment. The way Smith remembered it, it was Ruff who should have used more discretion and a better road map.

"Ruff deserved what he got," said Smith afterwards. "He wanted to be a hero, but he was a sucker instead. He was trying to run [charge] me, though he would never admit it. He skated up from behind and came this close (*Smith held up two fingers an inch apart*) to hitting me. Now, why would a guy have come within inches of my shoulder if he wasn't trying to run me? He had the whole ice to go up and down — the whole ice. So why did he have to come right on top of me? He didn't have to; that's the point. All I did was put my stick up to protect myself; I didn't go to hit him. In that situation if I really wanted to hurt him, I could have crucified the guy."

It was Smith who was subsequently crucified over l'Affaire Ruff, as well as his *contretemps* with the Great Gretzky. During an Oilers-Islanders match at Nassau Coliseum in 1981, the first shot in what evolved into an ongoing Smith-Gretzky serial was fired by Bad Bill. It started when the angular Edmonton ace loped behind the Islanders net, attempting either to deliver a pass or circle in front and fire point-blank at Smith. To cope with such forays, Smith had refined a neat gambit introduced in the 1940s by another eruptive goalie named Bill "Legs" Fraser. As his foe would deke behind the net, Fraser would whirl his stick boomerang-style over and behind the net with such speed that his startled opponent would be shocked into losing the puck.

Smith added a clever fillip to the Fraser plan. Instead of looping his stick over the net, Bill curled it around the right side with virtually the same results. In theory, the maneuver of trying to dislodge the puck from the enemy is no different for a goaltender than when a forward or defenseman attempts to annex the rubber, the difference being that the goaltender wields a larger club than his challengers.

In this instance, on the night of October 27, 1981, Gretzky crumbled behind the Islanders net when Smith's stick made contact with The Great One's leg. The contact was no more severe than that inflicted hundreds of other times by others checking the skinny center. Nevertheless, Gretzky was escorted from the ice never to return that evening. One might have thought that Gretzky was finished for the season but, in fact, he returned the next night to give one of his virtuoso performances as the Oilers trounced the New York Rangers. Nevertheless, the incident elicited so much invective from the media that NHL vice-president Brian O'Neill, the league's minister of misconduct, reviewed films of the collision and not only exonerated Smith, but added an off-the-cuff wrist-slapping for the media-types who had been trying to make a mountain out of an unorthodox backcheck.

Unfortunately, Smith's bluster and occasional blockbusting often beclouded the artistic part of his goaltending. He was as much a part of the Islanders four-straight Stanley Cup dynasty as anyone and underlined his worth by remaining a pivotal part of the team through the 1987-88 season. When the Islanders won the Patrick Division regular season title on April 2, 1988, Smith could take pride in the fact that he had played 38 games, allowing only 133 goals against for a respectable 3.22 goals-against average, and this at age 37. That same season, Smith's name was etched into the record book when he tied Turk Broda's record for 302 all-time career wins.

Smitty could never be placed on a plateau with Glenn Hall, Terry Sawchuk or Georges Vezina as one of "the very best" goaltenders because there were shortcomings in the technical aspects of his game. But William John Smith more than overcame those defects. And today, long after his retirement and enshrinement in the Hockey Hall of Fame, Smith is ranked among the best clutch goalies of all time.

-9-
Glen Hanlon

One of the most colorful goaltenders of the early 1980s, Glen Hanlon performed for a cavalcade of National Hockey League teams before continuing his career as goaltending advisor to the Vancouver Canucks.

Hanlon followed in a long line of belligerent netminders: Harry Lumley and Bill Smith, among others. Although he never performed for a Stanley Cup champion, he starred on a number of teams, including the Canucks and Detroit Red Wings.

Ask Glen and he'll confess that one of his most notable thrills was playing in a match that some regard as one of the finest playoff games of all time. This was the fifth and final game of the 1984 New York Rangers-New York Islanders best-of-five playoff at Nassau Coliseum.

Netminding for the Broadway Blueshirts, Hanlon faced "Battlin' Bill" Smith at the other end of the rink in the rubber game of the series. Both goaltenders were outstanding throughout the excruciatingly thrilling regulation time, which concluded with the teams still tied.

Hanlon, who deserved a better fate, finally was beaten by a long, screened shot fired by defenseman Ken Morrow. Like other aces of his ilk, Hanlon simply filed away the episode and continued to play his position as well as he could.

Now in a better position to reflect on his career, the redhead spoke with Vancouver reporter Sandra MacPherson about his past as well as the game today.

Q: You've been a goaltending coach for the Canucks for a couple of years now. Can we assume, therefore, that you can claim responsibility for Kirk McLean?

GH: No, I think when you get a hold of a goaltender who's already in his mid-20s, he's pretty much already formed his own patterns and style. It's already been predetermined for him. You have more influence with the kids who are 17 years old. What you do for the guys here is try to help them get through the times when the game is not so much fun. That can be because of many things. Either their teammates are not playing well for them and not giving them support, or the team just isn't winning or isn't being a sounding board. Mental support.

Q: Did you ever have that kind of a luxury while you were playing?

GH: Yeah, I did. I had it in New York where I worked with Wayne Thomas. To me, he is just one of the greatest guys that I've ever come across, as far as being a coach. He'd be able to read the individual, where if you had a night that you weren't too happy with he'd say, "Well, let's come tomorrow and do some work." You might not even go on the ice. You might just sit down and have a cup of coffee and talk about your golf game or whatever is on your mind. He certainly made it a lot easier. You can also work as a liaison to the other coaches who haven't had the experience of a goaltender. They might want to look at a fault or a problem and you might be able to alert them to something. You can also let the other coaches know what a goaltender wants in practice. That's how Wayne helped me.

Q: What about the time you spent in St. Louis when Emile Francis was there?

GH: Yeah, but he wasn't involved to that degree. He was a general manager and a governor and a coach. Almost the same capacity of what Pat [Quinn] is. Obviously when you get that busy you can't take one person and work with them on something. It's absolutely impossible. Plus, that was in '82. I went to the Rangers in '83-'84. There was another year when the goaltending coaches were just starting to come into effect.

Q: Let's talk about young Glen, growing up in Brandon, Manitoba. Living here in Vancouver, my impression of Brandon is some small town on the icy prairie where it snows 11 months out of the year. I guess it would be pretty natural for you then to take up hockey. Why goal? What was the attraction?

GH: I don't really know. I can't really think why. I just kind of ended up there. Possibly because I was so young when I started out that I couldn't really skate, so they put me out there. I had an older brother who had four years on me and he could skate so he probably just stuck me in goal and I stayed there ever since. As far as that happening nowadays, for kids, without the access of outdoor rinks where you can do something like that, with organized hockey starting at six or seven years old, by then you're formulating some sort of ideas. You've got some feelings as to what position that you want to play, what with role models and local stars.

Q: Did you ever play outdoors?

GH: Oh yeah. All the time.

Q: Well, tell me what that was like. Remember, I'm from the west coast where we all whine about zero degree temperatures as opposed to the minus 30s that you used to get in Brandon.

GH: Well, we couldn't play indoors until we were something like 11 years old. I remember it being so cold that school was called off and then we'd go to the outdoor rink and play hockey. Whenever you'd hear that it was so cold or there was a certain wind-chill factor and the schools would close, we'd just head over to the rink. So it wasn't a deterrent. It was a bonus. So when it gets down to freezing here and I get cold, I wonder how the heck we used to do it as kids. You certainly became oblivious to the cold. Maybe you were just enjoying yourself so much. You'd go out and play and then you'd go inside where we had this shack where we'd get changed and that. Then we'd play hockey out there. Mind you, now I think things are changing. I think in Brandon there's something like five indoor rinks. I don't know if it's good or bad.

Q: Now, growing up as a young guy, I don't imagine you were fully outfitted as far as gear goes.

GH: I had everything. My family wasn't very well off, but I was very fortunate. My father always saw that I had all the very best equipment. I owe a lot to my family. They always saw that I was well equipped.

Q: When did you start to get serious about hockey?

GH: I think at about 14.

Q: So, at that point you felt you had a chance to go somewhere with it.

GH: Yes. I think at that age you're starting to realize you're maybe one of the better players on the team. You're starting to get some invitations to go to junior hockey camps at that age. You're starting to understand that your dreams are beginning to become goals. I think you begin to realize the sacrifices that you have to make to attain those goals.

Q: Was there anyone in particular who encouraged you?

GH: Not really encourage, more support. Obviously from your family you get support. As far as encouraging, or making it a must to go down to the rink, it was never really that environment.

Q: You played Junior for the Brandon Wheat Kings and at that time players were groomed a lot differently than they are today. It was still the last remnants of the "If you can beat 'em in the alley" era. Here in the Vancouver area we had a particularly tough team with the New Westminster Bruins with the likes of coach Punch McLean and players Stan Smyl and Barry Beck. What was it like coming into a building as notorious as Queens Park Arena?

GH: Well, I would say it was intimidating. I had the luxury of having a mask on the whole game and having the support of your teammates. It was very intimidating for a lot of the players. The Bruins era was just incredible. Just the amount of success that they had. And they had a lot of success with a lot less talented teams, but they really stressed the concept of all for one and one for all. Which I agree with. I could certainly admire what Ernie [McLean] and Stan and those guys had done. Mind you, now the rules wouldn't allow for quite that type of environment. I think that there was a lot of publicity over the brawls during the four- or five-year period, but you forget about the good, solid tough hockey that we try to get our guys to play. Good, solid checking and good, physical contact. Never trying to avoid any form of physical contact. We as ex-players and fans tend to forget that and just focus on the brawls as years go by.

Q: I seem to recall a story that you told one time about coming into New Westminster and having the Bruins players steal your pucks during the warmup.

GH: We had one game in the playoffs where we would all line up at the red line and they kept taking our pucks. So we lost that game. So we had a meeting after the game and the whole focus wasn't on what we had to do to win the next day, but that we weren't going to let them take our pucks in warmup. We had ended up with one puck and everybody was trying to get a shot with this one puck. It ended up that this one guy stood up and said, "The first puck that goes into their zone, I'm going to get it." So next game, we're all waiting and then the first puck goes in and he goes in to get it and the Bruins are all shooting pucks at this guy and he had to high-tail it back into our end. So we kind of distanced ourselves from them and tried to guard our pucks as best we could. The obvious side of that story that people can take as a negative is being goons or whatever, but there is a deep, deep motto there that this is our building and we're going to rule our building. No one is going to come into our building and show us how to do it. Consequently, you get players who are maybe less timid than they should be and they end up being some of the aggressors. Within the rules I think it's a good concept as long as no one gets hit with a stick.

Q: This next question might be a little long-winded, but it's kind of a two-parter. I remember the first NHL game that I saw in this building with the Canucks and the Philadelphia Flyers. The Flyers had Bobby Clarke, Reggie Leach, Andre DuPont, Bill Barber, Dave Schultz, etc. That game ended up being the highest penalty-filled game in the NHL (344 min., Feb. 24, 1980) at that time. Part two: A Canuck yearbook described you as, "Sunny disposition disappears when opposing forward lingers in his crease." Now the question is, did you incite that brawl when one of the Flyers lingered a bit too long in your crease?

GH: No, I really didn't. I think there is a line there that they cross over. What I try to tell our goaltenders is that they've given all the forwards the whole 200' x 88', and we get 4' x 6' and we have to defend this crease. We have to defend this little, tiny crease, not in a physical manner but in an aggressive sense — we don't want to retreat on someone coming in. I certainly wasn't a Billy Smith. In fact, if I hit someone with my stick it would upset me so much that I would be wishing that I hadn't done that and would be focusing too much on that instead of the game. But I think there's a certain time where if they take away too much of what you're trying to defend, you have to stick up for your rights. All the goalies that I've had, I've tried to instill that type of behavior. Not where you're getting into fighting and pushing, but defending your area.

Q: Has the advent of a larger crease given goaltenders a better opportunity to showcase their talents then?

GH: They do, but as a goalie I don't like the way the game has gone offensively. It's almost like in baseball where every rule is structured to favor the hitter. In offense, the same thing applies to the goaltender. They've brought back four-on-four play. All the different rules and equipment changes seem to favor offense. Everything is so much faster. Pre-scouting is just so much more difficult for a goaltender to shine year in year out. It's incredible. The only rule that they've brought in is the protection of the goaltenders. And still, I don't think that's called as much as it should be. I mean, they are so vulnerable even with all the equipment. You are so focused on the puck you can't see anybody coming in at you, so obviously you're going to get hurt pretty bad.

Q: Do you remember one particular instance where you got hit during the play?

GH: I remember one time when I went to handle the puck in Montreal and I turned around and Bob Gainey hit me. I don't think it was on purpose. I just turned and skated right into him. I remember it was so hard I said I'm glad I'm in goal. I don't care what anybody says. If I had to get hit like that the whole game, year in, year out, I don't think I could take it. I'd rather get hit by a little, wee puck going 80 mph rather than a 200-pound forward going 30 mph. So I was a lot happier in my net. And it was a good lesson because I was a little more aware of where I was going and what I was doing with the puck from then on.

Q: Were you with Vancouver at the time?

GH: Yes.

Q: First year you played in the NHL, 1977-78, you played four games, but the minute totals actually come to three games and 20 minutes. I want to focus on that 20 minutes. Were the 20 minutes the first time you stepped on the ice?

GH: No. What happened was, right at the end of the season we were trying to make the playoffs and I had played against Philadelphia and we tied that game 3-3. My next game was against St. Louis and we won that 4-2. We had two games left and it was a tough decision for our coach Orland Kurtenbach, because we'd gotten into a position where we had to win our last two games and we played against Los Angeles. Caesar Maniago started and played the first two periods and unfortunately for him, and fortunately for me, I got to play the third period and then the last game in L.A. So that's where the 20 minutes came from.

Q: What was your first NHL experience like?

GH: It was great. In youth you'd never experienced any real form of defeat or any bad stretches or anything like that up until then. So, to make it to the NHL you've been one of the better players all your life. I'd played in the minor leagues, so you're still on a level where you experience success. So coming in you really have no recollection of what it's like to taste failure. Absolutely, just the excitement of it was phenomenal. To put that jersey on for the first time was just so exciting. It's not until you get burned a few times or take a month and a half where you're not doing so great that it makes playing so difficult.

Q: The first team you started against was Philadelphia, as you mentioned. You were told you were going to start. Tell me the feelings you had at the time.

GH: I remember I was going from Tulsa to Vancouver and I couldn't get into Vancouver. I had trouble in Seattle, I can't remember why. I remember I had to rent a car to get the final leg. I remember talking to Larry Popein on the phone out of the Seattle airport and he said I had to get up there because he was pretty sure I would be starting the next day. I never really thought of it until then. I just thought I was going up, I didn't think I would be playing.

Q: How were you on game days?

GH: Well, I changed. When I started out I used to be pretty reclusive, but eventually I was doing everything I could to go out and talk to people. You realize that you have to play within your personality. You have to adapt. You can't just do the same thing year in, year out. I used to think about the game from the moment the alarm went off in the morning at 8 a.m. until the game was over. But eventually, I was able to work it up to 6:00 at night where I would turn it on and focus. Obviously, I would have a little bit of thought here and there, but not preplanned thoughts. That's what I try to encourage our goalies to do. The later you can go in the day to think about the game, the better off you are. You don't wear yourself out as much.

Q: Did you get into a routine on game days or have any superstitions?

GH: All the time. I don't think that they were superstitions. I just think that they were the way that you do things. You have little checkpoints during the day that if you're mentally sharp those things are taken care of. You know that if at 11:00 you normally are getting your sticks ready for the game, if you don't do that, I wouldn't think, "Uh oh. I'm going to play bad tonight." I know that that's part of my job at 11:00. Part of my pre-game routine. If I'm not doing that, then I have to focus in here and get my train of thought going. Now that's worrying about my game. That's not at 11:00 going, "tonight I have to face Shutt or Lafleur." That's just mentally sharpening yourself.

Q: You played with a few guys during your career. Do you know of any superstitions any of them may have had? Greg Stefan used to be a little superstitious, wasn't he?

GH: Greg used to carry some things. What the heck did he have? Oh, he had an octopus. Someone sent him a stuffed octopus. Of course, the legend in Detroit was with the octopus on the ice. Someone had thrown him an octopus, so he would carry that around. Actually, the goalies that I played with were some pretty normal guys. Greg Stefan was probably one of the most even-keeled guys in the sense of not worrying about superstitions. I played with Mike Liut, who was a very intelligent guy. Richard Brodeur was the type of guy to whom nothing really mattered. He'd just go out and play at 8:00. John Vanbiesbrouk was a pretty intelligent guy, too. So all the goalies I played with were pretty normal guys. Some people think that putting your equipment on a certain way is a superstition, but to me that's too obvious. It's just the way you get ready. Kind of like the way you'd get ready for work in the morning. You probably put one shoe on before you put on the other. Just a certain routine that you do things.

Q: You played with Gary Bromley. He had that great mask.

GH: Yeah, Gary was another great guy. He had that skeleton mask. I think there is a persona about goalies being a little wacko. I think that there are a few who are, but I'll tell you that there are lots of forwards who do some pretty wild things. I mean, I can always remember lots of forwards coming up and wanting to hit you with their sticks a certain way, or hit here or there. You're just trying to get them out of the way so you can worry about the game. And they're banging posts and doing their little pre-game dance and things. I think they're just as superstitious as we are.

Q: Glenn Hall once said that goaltending is 60 minutes of hell. Did you ever experience that?

GH: Well, you do. You're constantly faced with being one shot away from embarrassing yourself in front of so many people. I don't miss the pressure of playing everyday. When you're playing you enjoy it, but when it's over, you go, "holy mackerel." You see a guy like Kirk McLean. I wish I could have lived my life and played with the composure that he does. On the other hand, Kirk is a very, very talented player and for the top four or five in the league they have the luxury of being that good. They have a whole bunch of wins under their belt. It's like gambling. It's a lot easier to gamble when you've already won a bunch of money. So, when you're a goaltender who's not in the top ten of the league, every game has a lot more importance to it. So, it's very, very difficult. Very, *very* difficult.

Q: Before I ask you about your days in New York, tell me again about your first game in the NHL. I know you came up from Tulsa and then traveled up to Vancouver from Seattle to make it up for the next game. But what was the feeling, the atmosphere like in the dressing room?

GH: It was a good atmosphere. At the time, we had quite a few guys who had been called up from Tulsa. Lots of guys that I had played with in Tulsa. We had one guy in particular, Claire Alexander, who was just a really good guy. A real team guy who was at the end of his career here. As a matter of fact, it might have even been his last year here in North America. He just said, "Come and do the things here that you did down there." It was really reassuring. We had a good captain at the time, Chris Oddleifson.

Q: About New York. You were traded there from St. Louis and, as you said, you didn't have the luxury of a goaltending coach until you reached the Rangers. Was your personality such that you would still get pretty wound up prior to the games?

GH: Yes, yes. It wasn't until then, when I started to spend some time with Wayne Thomas, that we sort of made some changes. The way he went about it, I didn't really even know there was a transformation taking place with my personality and the playing mechanics. As it worked out, he extended my career by about seven years, for sure.

Q: So he just got you to relax.

GH: Just relax a lot more and enjoy every day. To work on your fundamentals, day in, day out. Always gain confidence, and have good fundamentals.

Q: Tell me about the fans in New York. I remember a time here in Vancouver when the Canucks were playing Boston and Pete Peeters was in goal. A fan jumped over the glass with his skates on while play was continuing and skated in on Peeters and scored a goal. Did you have any odd kind of things like that that ever occurred?

GH: The thing about New York fans, as has been said before, is that they're the best of the best and the worst of the worst. And when things are going well, there may be no better place to play. But on nights when things aren't going well they can be pretty critical. But overall, I had really no complaints. It was tough at first. I think there is a period where you have to show to the fans that you are worth their dollar and their time to come out. That you deserve to wear the blue, red and white of the Rangers. It takes a while, but once they accept you it's a great experience.

Q: What about booing?

GH: I don't care what anybody says, it affects you. When it's really bad and you've got 17,000 people screaming at you, for someone to say that it doesn't bother you, they are just trying to pull the wool over your eyes. You can't help it, let it bother you. I was fortunate. It wasn't that bad. I had a lot of good nights in there. Sure, there were some bad nights where frustration of the fans would come out against you. But overall, really not a lot of complaints.

Q: Did you ever lose your cool with a fan?

GH: No, I never did. I was fortunate enough. As a goaltender you're not in around them that much. Except when you're going off the ice, but then you're always in the middle of a bunch of guys. On the road, you're completely covered. So you don't have much chance to come into contact with them.

Q: Ever been in a building where people begin to throw things at the player on the ice?

GH: Yeah, my first game in St. Louis when I got traded there. We lost 7-0. It was frisbee night and everyone started throwing their frisbees at me! My whole end of the ice was covered. But, besides that, I don't think that we can't handle getting hit with a frisbee. I don't think that can hurt.

Q: Well, that was a real how-do-you-do, to St. Louis.

GH: Yes. Certainly when I didn't even want to be there at the time. I still wanted to be in Vancouver. It wasn't a lot of fun.

Q: Were you part of the Rangers when Bob MacCammon infamously referred to them as smurfs?

GH: Yes.

Q: What was that like? That must really pump a team up to hear that.

GH: Well, we had a good game plan at that time. We were small and we felt our only means of intimidation was the power play. We were told not to fight and we had no means of intimidating their team physically. But we had guys like Mark Pavelich, Rejio Routsalainen and Anders Hedberg. A lot of very skilled players. We took everything. We took a lot of hits in the head, a lot of checks from behind and that. But our power play, I think, won us the series. We won it in three straight games that year, I think. It was a learning experience for me. At the time Herb Brooks was the coach and it really made me understand that you coach the team that you have and you can't let your personality or your beliefs dictate how you're going to coach. Those are my feelings. If you have a bunch of talented players, you can't tell them to go out and fight every night. They won't be playing to their strengths. Herbie really taught me a lot that year.

Q: Your stay in New York probably offered you the best of times and the worst of times. And if there was one game that really summed that up for you, it would be '83-'84 Stanley Cup finals. Fifth game in the semis, versus the four-time Cup winners, New York Islanders. Cross-town rivals.

GH: Yeah, that was very disheartening at the time. But when you look back on it, I was involved in probably one of the top games. As a matter of fact, I remember seeing a rating of the all-time playoff games and that game was in there. I can't remember where it was rated, but it was pretty high. It was really, really exciting when I look back on it. Unfortunately, we didn't win. At the time, it was my first real exposure to playoffs. I was playing against Billy Smith, who maybe is the greatest all-time goaltender in playoffs. That was one of the highlights in my whole career. Something that I will always remember from that series is this: Billy was notorious as a real competitor who would never shake hands and at the end of the game, when we skated off the ice, he tapped me on the pads. Even in defeat, there was something that came out of that series that I will take with me forever. It was such a small gesture, but to me, I got beat by someone who was better than myself and who had more success and went on to have even more success. To me, that was a victory.

Q: Also, during your career, you suffered a lot of injuries and this certainly silenced the critics as to whether or not you had the right stuff to be a good goalie.

GH: Basically what happened — I don't know if Wayne Thomas was directly responsible or if it was Craig Patrick — but, before I arrived in New York, they had Ed Mio the year before and he had had a good year. They had Steve Weeks there. They had made a decision to trade a goalie and they traded Ed Mio away. I came there January 14th or something like that. They made a commitment to me and it was a great feeling. Once again, I'm grateful to people like that who gave me the chance.

Q: You must have heard the "1940" chant when you played there. What was that like?

GH: It doesn't bother you. I had only been there a couple of years. That's something that they just do. I don't think it really affects you one way or the other.

Q: What about the injuries?

GH: Well, the injuries came early. With two shoulder operations and two knee injuries, you learn that the game is very important to you. You have lots of time off and have plenty of time to think. When you think you may not play again you have a new outlook on your career. That happened to me and certainly having an opportunity to play again after those injuries, you enjoy every single day that you receive.

Q: The injuries — was there ever one that was so disappointing you felt as though you just wanted to hang them up?

GH: After my second shoulder. After I had had trouble with the first and then the second. I just said, "Boy, I don't know if this is even worth it."

Q: Where did it happen?

GH: It happened here, in Vancouver. Our doctor was good. After I had hurt it, we went back to his house that night and had a couple of drinks of rum. And after a couple of drinks of rum we said, "Oh well. We'll be okay. We'll get over it."

Q: How did it happen?

GH: I think I just fell on it and it just popped out.

Q: Quite painful, I imagine.

GH: Actually not bad. You just knew there was no strength, so there was something wrong.

Q: Was it the worst?

GH: I would think so, yes.

Q: You were traded a few times. What was the worst?

GH: Vancouver, without a doubt. That was the only trade that really affected me. The other ones, I had been asked to be traded from St. Louis. Then the one in New York, there were other goalies there that were going to play and I was going to a great organization in Detroit, so I was happy.

Q: I guess by that time you had matured to a degree so it wasn't as disappointing, as opposed to when you were quite young and being drafted by the Canucks.

GH: Well, it was your first team and you have an allegiance. It was unfortunate that I wasn't here my whole career, but I was able to go around and experience all the other teams. I wouldn't have it any other way. You realize what we have here and how lucky we are, the city we have. It was a great experience. Now to be back and pursue that commitment to win the Stanley Cup in Vancouver has made my career complete.

Q: What about rumors? Were there teams that you definitely didn't want to go to?

GH: No, not really. Not really. I had always wanted to play for the

Toronto Maple Leafs because I had always wanted to see what it was like.

Q: Even though it was during the infamous Harold Ballard years?

GH: Yeah. There was something about the Toronto Maple Leafs and the Montreal Canadiens. You just wanted to see what it was like in those dressing rooms and to wear that sweater and to do those things. Those were a couple of teams that I would have liked to have played for. I got to play for two of the original six in New York and Detroit. It's pretty tough to beat playing for them.

Q: Finally, despite all of the things that you have experienced in your career, like it or not, you will always be remembered for the possibility of becoming a question on a Trivial Pursuit card. "Who was the goaltender who Wayne Gretzky scored his first goal on?"

GH: Yeah. So when you look back and you've played for 14 years and you're a goalie and you're famous for a goal that you let in, maybe it says something about your career!

-10-
Glenn Hall

NOVEMBER 7, 1962:
Chicago netminder Glenn Hall's streak of 502 complete games comes to a close.

Mention to a contemporary hockey fan that a National Hockey League goaltender once played more than 500 consecutive games without a mask and no doubt that person would do a double — if not a triple — take.

In the game of the 1990s, the chances of a netminder stringing together 500 straight matches is roughly equivalent to Tie Domi winning the Art Ross Trophy as the game's leading scorer.

Yet, on November 7, 1962, Chicago's Glenn Hall — having played his 502nd consecutive complete game three nights before in a 3-1 loss at Detroit — anchored himself in the Chicago Stadium nets for No. 503.

As fate would have it, however, Hall would be physically unable to finish the game. He had suffered a pinched nerve in his back during the Blackhawks morning practice and was forced off the ice during the first period as Chicago and the Boston Bruins skated to a 3-3 tie.

While Hall's accomplishment is mind-boggling in its own right, the NHL-record streak of 502 complete games becomes even more unfathomable when considering the fact that Hall also faced the rather distasteful, potentially health-impairing chore of going up against teammate Bobby "The Golden Jet" Hull in about 500-plus practices.

Perhaps that explains why Blackhawks fans tabbed Hall "Mister Goalie," although he opened his career with the Detroit Red Wings in 1952 and closed it with the St. Louis Blues in 1971. How did he do it? As Hall admits, it wasn't easy.

"Before every game, and sometimes between periods, I'd get sick to my stomach. I'd have to throw up," Hall remembers. "Sometimes it happened during a game and I'd have to fight it off

48

until the whistle blew. I tried drinking tea between periods and that seemed to help. But I didn't worry about it. Nervousness is part of the game. It helped keep me sharp."

But how did he do it? How did he fashion a career that few have surpassed either in terms of wins or longevity? With creativity: by inventing a totally new style of puckstopping.

At the time Hall pushed his way into the NHL, there were only six teams in the league and each of them had a goalkeeper who essentially employed a rather basic system for preventing the puck from entering the net.

"They used what we call the 'stand-up style,'" recalls New Jersey scout Bob Bellemore, the Devils former goalie coach. "Shots were getting harder and harder and the 'screen' was coming into vogue, so Terry Sawchuk [Hall's predecessor in Detroit] came up with what was then a new idea — crouching so he could see between the legs of the screening players."

The Sawchuk Crouch was considered a major advance in the goaltending art — until Hall came along. Not only did Hall come along, but he managed to do to Sawchuk what Sawchuk had done to Hall-of-Famer Harry Lumley before him: replace the big guy as Detroit's starting goalie.

Like Lumley and Sawchuk, Hall was a product of General Manager Jack Adams' vast Red Wings farm system. Sawchuk had been a whizkid with Indianapolis and simply had to be promoted. Result: Lumley was dealt to Chicago. Then, as Yogi Berra would say, "It was deja-vu all over again." Hall took over at Indianapolis and produced such prodigious netminding feats that Adams had no choice but to give him a chance. So long, Sawchuk — to the Boston Bruins.

Hall also took over Sawchuk's role as innovator by introducing an improvement to the Sawchuk Crouch. At the time, it was considered *de rigueur* for goalies to do a ballet-type split in order to protect the two corners of the net. But it was not fashionable to drop to one's knees. In fact, the knee-drop was considered particularly vulnerable and, in the eyes of purists, gauche as goaltenders go. Hall changed all that.

Back then, his creation was called the "Inverted V" (as in Victory), and is now known as "The Butterfly" technique. Mister Goalie would drop to the ice a split-second after the shot was taken and fan out his legs to the left and right.

Viewed from the rear, it looked like an upside-down letter V. Viewed from the front by a shooter, it looked like a formidable barrier. There was, however, a trick to the maneuver.

Hockey sages, starting with the immortal Lester Patrick, had counseled against goalies going to their knees on the grounds that they left themselves vulnerable; that they would soon be unable to get vertical soon enough to stop a rebound. Hall took care of that problem by digging his blade points into the ice when going down into the Inverted V so that he could instantly push off on them and spring up into a standing position if necessary. Thus, he was protected from all angles.

"The system worked," adds Bellemore. "Hall proved that."

But as it turned out, the system wouldn't be enough to keep him in a Red Wings jersey. Ironically, Jack Adams considered Hall — the man who would tend goal in the NHL for 500-plus consecutive games — to be too timid.

"We were playing Boston," says Hall, "and I got flattened by a shot by Vic Stasiuk. Right in the face."

In the 1950s, teams did not carry spare goaltenders. Unless the chief puckstopper bordered on the brink of death, he was expected to return, no matter how devastating or messy the injury. And this happened to be a bad one. Taken from the ice on a stretcher, Hall regained consciousness in the trainer's room. A full 23 stitches were required to return his lips and mouth to usable shape.

"What was uppermost in your mind in those days," says Hall, "was survival. You knew there was a guy on the farm team waiting to take your job, so you made darn sure that, if it was humanly possible, you'd stay in that net."

And he did. A half-hour after being felled, Hall emerged from the infirmary, his eyes black, his face swollen and covered with bandages. It was evident to 15,000 fans that only a heavy tank — and even that was debatable — could dislodge him from the crease.

But Adams was unmoved. The crusty Red Wings boss believed that his goalie had been at least partially traumatized by l'Affaire Stasiuk, and privately confided to aides that Hall was "puck-shy," just about the ultimate put-down for a netminder.

Not only that, but Adams followed through in July, 1957, by trading Hall to Chicago, which was: 1) the best thing that ever happened to the Blackhawks; 2) the best thing that ever happened to Glenn Hall; and 3) the move needed for Chicago to win its first (and last) post-World War II Stanley Cup in 1961.

"I didn't like Jack Adams and he didn't like me," Hall allows. "When we lost to Boston in the playoffs, he came into the dressing room and said it was my fault. So, then he traded me to Chicago and when I did well with the Blackhawks, what do you think Adams said? He said that he was doing the Hawks a favor by trading me to them."

A curious marriage of ballet's Baryshnikov and Hollywood's Robocop in terms of style and durability, Hall played game after game and got better and better. Perhaps the fact that teammate Bobby Hull had developed hockey's hardest, most devastating shot actually helped, because The Golden Jet would unleash the rubber at Hall in practice after practice.

"It was tough facing Bobby," Hall chuckles. "He was such a brash kid and a little wild with his shots. But as he got older he began to take it easier on me."

The Blackhawks were loaded with future Hall of Famers such as Hull, Stan Mikita and Pierre Pilote, yet they were a difficult club for a goaltender because it remained an offense-oriented, basically undisciplined outfit. Hall never complained, but he did admit that the job was filled with anxiety.

"Goalkeeping is a strain. You're tired and fed up with the game at the end of the season. The feeling lasts until about the first of July. Then you just can't wait to get back. Believe me, there are easier ways to make a living."

The Blackhawks brass was acutely aware of Hall's vulnerability as he surpassed the 200 consecutive game mark, then the 300-straight-game milepost and headed for 400. General Manager Tommy Ivan had developed an impressive farm system in St. Catharines, Ontario, and Buffalo of the American Hockey League. From there he discovered a superb goalie named Denis DeJordy.

"There was no doubt that DeJordy was being groomed to replace Hall," says veteran New York sportscaster Bill Mazer, who worked in Buffalo at that time. "You had to see DeJordy to believe him. He was every bit as good as Sawchuk in his prime and every bit as good as Hall when Glenn played in the minors. It was simply a matter of Hall faltering. The moment that happened — and Ivan became convinced that Glenn was permanently losing it — Hall would be traded just as Sawchuk had been before him and DeJordy would become the Blackhawks number one goalie."

Unfortunately for DeJordy, there was a hitch: Hall wouldn't cooperate. If anything, he improved as his consecutive game streak got longer and longer. "He was solid in every way," says Andy Bathgate, a Hall of Famer who started with the New York Rangers. "Glenn had a great pair of hands and he played those angles. He was smart, awfully smart, and kept on getting better."

Meanwhile, DeJordy waited. It wasn't until the 1962-63 season that Denis got his break. By that time, Hall had played complete seasons (every single game without a break) from 1955-56 through 1961-62. He totaled more than 30,000 successive minutes of goaltending before DeJordy finally moved between the pipes.

"Even then," Mazer recalls, "Hall refused to wilt. DeJordy only played in five games in 1962-63 and six the following year. By this time, teams like the Maple Leafs [with Johnny Bower, Don Simmons and Terry Sawchuk] would be using a two-goalie system."

It wasn't until the 1964-65 season that Hall began to ease up on his workload, playing 41 games that season. But he remained the primary Chicago goalie until he was claimed by the St. Louis Blues in the first expansion draft.

In 1967-68, Hall played spectacularly as St. Louis upset Philadelphia in seven games to reach the Stanley Cup finals against Montreal. "Strangely enough," Hall concludes, "I found St. Louis the easiest team of all to play with and that goes back to the good Detroit and Chicago clubs. We had a very disciplined defense with Scotty Bowman coaching, and a stronger defense than we had in Chicago.

"Besides that, we were motivated. Players on expansion teams in those days really wanted to prove to the world that they were good enough to play in the NHL."

As a Blue, Hall had the good fortune of sharing netminding duties with Jacques Plante for a time. Ironically, Plante was the goalie who popularized the face mask and yet, even in St. Louis, Hall eschewed the protective device.

It was only during the final half of the 1970-71 season, at the very end of his career — when virtually every goaltender had retreated behind a mask — that Hall relented and donned the mask, but he never felt very comfortable with it.

By the time he retired, Hall had played in 906 regular season games and 115 playoff contests for a total of 60,363 minutes. He captured the Calder Trophy as Rookie of the Year in 1956, the Conn Smythe Trophy as Playoff MVP in 1968, three Vezina Trophies as the league's top goalie, and seven First All-Star Team selections. He also led the NHL in shutouts six times, finishing with 84 for his career.

Truly, he was Mister Goalie.

-11-
Johnny Bower: THE OLDEST GUY IN THE FASTEST GAME

Even among old-timers, Johnny Bower was a throwback. A product of The Great Depression, Bower grew up in rural Saskatchewan under the most primitive of circumstances. Despite an absence of riches, Bower was able to learn the goaltending profession well enough to make his way to the pro ranks.

It was then that his career took one of the most curious turns imaginable. He played brilliantly for Cleveland in the American Hockey League and finally won his way to the National Hockey League's New York Rangers in 1953.

Although the Broadway Blueshirts were a dreadful club, Bower kept them playoff-afloat until the final weeks of the season when they finished in fifth place. Nevertheless, Johnny posted a handsome 2.60 goals-against average which should have guaranteed him a long career in New York.

The fickle finger of fate had other ideas. Instead of retaining Bower, the Rangers shipped him back to the AHL and promoted young Lorne "Gump" Worsley in his place. It appeared that at age 30, Bower had seen the last of the bigs.

Ever the warrior, Johnny played magnificently in the AHL; well enough to earn the respect and attention of George "Punch" Imlach who would soon become general manager and coach of the Toronto Maple Leafs.

After Imlach was promoted himself to the NHL in 1958, he immediately sought Bower as the Toronto goaltender and, at age 34 , Johnny proceeded to prove why the Rangers had made a terrible mistake and why he would eventually — along with Worsley, incidentally — be named to The Hockey Hall of Fame.

Bower was one of the primary reasons why Imlach's Leafs evolved into an NHL dynasty as he helped them to Stanley Cup triumphs in 1962, 1963, 1964 and 1967. Just happy to play goal, Bower never enjoyed the riches of contemporary netminders but he never complained either. He remained in the Leafs system after his retirement as a player and, as goaltending coach, was regarded as one of the best.

Still a resident of Toronto , Bower chatted about all aspects of his career with reporter Eric Martin, himself a goaltender and close friend of Johnny. The following is vintage John Bower.

Things were pretty tough for us when I was a kid, growing up in Prince Albert (Saskatchewan). My family didn't even have enough money to buy me a pair of skates.

What I did was go out on the ponds and rivers with just a pair of boots on looking for a game. I wound up in goal because none of the other kids wanted to stop pucks and that's how my career all started.

It was nothing fancy back in those Depression years. We used a couple of cans for goal posts and whacked the puck back and forth. Even as a kid I would dream about playing in the NHL. Every Saturday night I would turn on the radio and listen to Foster Hewitt broadcast the Maple Leaf games. I could hardly wait until Toronto played Boston because my favorite goaltender was Frankie Brimsek of the Boston Bruins. I loved his nickname, Mister Zero, and he was the reason why I always had an ambition to play for Boston.

By the time I had made it to the church hockey league, my mother was gone and my father thought that hockey was too rough of a game for me. He told me to go to school, that's all. But I'd do my homework and then go out in the 45- and 50-degree below zero weather and play goal. It's way cold in Prince Albert.

Now that may seem strange — just standing there while the other fellas are skating around, but I used to watch the defensemen and forwards get bounced around, knocked down and get back up again and here I am standing there. I figured, heck, I got it better than they do. At least I'm still standing on my feet.

Getting a pair of goalie pads was another story. Buying them was out of the question because we just didn't have the money. One day the kid next door got an idea and made me a pair of goal pads out of a mattress. I found that better than using the old Eaton's catalogues.

We couldn't even afford pucks so my dad would find an eight-foot piece of lumber and cut pieces of wood the size of a hockey puck. When we ran out of the wooden pucks we'd follow the horses around in the winter and use their droppings for pucks. They froze solid and we called them road apples.

It couldn't have hurt me too much because I kept improving and the next thing I knew I was playing for money in the American League for the Cleveland Barons. They were owned by a guy named Al Sutphin and run by a fellow named Jim Hendy who really was a solid hockey man. Our coach was Bun Cook, who had been left wing on the great early Rangers teams on a line with his brother, Bill, and Frank Boucher.

Bun helped my career a great deal. He was the kind of coach who would stay out on the ice and work with you. He'd fire shots, watch what I was doing and give me advice. One of the main things Cook taught me was to come out of the net a bit and cut down the angle. Up until that point in my career, nobody had ever mentioned the word angle to me. I didn't even know what he was talking about.

"C'mon out of the net a bit more," he would say.

When I heard that, I told Bun, "If I come out any further, I'm gonna get lost."

He said that I wouldn't get lost and that's how I became an angle goalie.

In the early 1950s, when I was having some good years with Cleveland, the NHL still was a six-team league and even the NHL teams carried only one goalie, so there wasn't the kind of opportunity there is today. But I didn't mind; the AHL was a very strong league at that time. Every club was sponsored by an NHL team and if it was 1994 then, every one of them would have been strong enough to be in the majors.

Even though my club, the Barons, was independent, Jim Hendy would occasionally sell some of our better players to the NHL clubs. Hendy liked to deal with Frank Boucher, who was manager of the Rangers, and had already sent Hy Buller to New York. I think he made the Second All-Star Team in his second year as a defenseman. The Rangers also got Steve Kraftcheck from Cleveland and Wally Hergesheimer, who became New York's best scorer for a while, and they got me for the 1953-54 season.

It was a strange year in a lot of ways. Toronto had figured that their one-time star center Max Bentley was through, so they sold him to New York. Max had lost quite a bit, but he still was a great point man on the power play. When he was well enough to play, Max was sensational. But there were lots of times when he didn't play. In mid-season we were losing games when Boucher got a bright idea. Max's older brother, Doug, was player-coach of the Saskatoon club in the Western League. Frank remembered when Max and Doug were teammates on the Chicago Blackhawks back in the mid-1940s, and how they, with Bill Mosienko, made up The Pony Line, one of the best in history.

Boucher talked Doug into coming back to the NHL and rejoining Max with the Rangers. This was a sensational story for its time and got great space in the papers. The night Doug arrived at Madison Square Garden, we were to play the Bruins, the team that was challenging us for fourth place, which was the last playoff berth.

There was a great crowd at the Garden that night and they weren't disappointed.

Max and Doug played on a line with another old-timer, Edgar Laprade, and they were sensational. We beat Boston, 8-3, and between them, Max and Doug wound up with around seven points. That game put us in the playoff hunt and we stayed close until the middle of March when Max and Doug just tired out and Boston passed us for good.

I ended the season with a 2.60 goals-against average and thought I'd stay with the Rangers, but the following year I was sent down to the minors and they brought up Gump Worsley to fill my place. It wasn't exactly good news, but I was sent down to Providence, which was a Rangers farm team in the AHL and we won a few Calder Cups there.

After that, I finally got my break with the Leafs, which was a very interesting team at the time. Punch Imlach had taken over and he mixed a bunch of young guys like Carl Brewer, Bob Baun, Bob Pulford and Billy Harris with some sharp veterans, including Red Kelly, Allan Stanley and Al Arbour.

Toronto beat the Rangers out for a playoff berth with a terrific run in the last two weeks of the 1958-59 season. The Leafs were behind by about seven or so points with only two weeks left and beat New York out on the final night. From that point on, we just took off and got better and better. By 1962 we had won the Stanley Cup.

Winning in that tough NHL really was an accomplishment because the league was full of stars. Chicago had won the Cup in 1961 with fellas like Bobby Hull, Stan Mikita and Glenn Hall. The Canadiens had the great Jean Beliveau and, of course, Gordie Howe was in his prime with Detroit.

What was it like to play against Gordie Howe?

He was a very, very strong skater and built like Superman. His arms were immense and he had a tremendous shot. You name it, he would fire it. He didn't bring his stick way back the way they do today, but he did it a little bit, slapped the thing and it went right in. He was very smart with the puck and all elbows. Boy, you got in the corner with him and look out! You'd get an elbow from him all the time. Gordie was a great competitor and leader for his team. Nobody wanted to fight with Gordie because once he got hold of you — he was like Tim Horton who played for our Leaf team — he'd squeeze until you would turn purple.

The other amazing thing about Gordie was his ambidexterity. He could switch hands with his stick and shoot from either side. Nobody else in the league could do that. I can remember him skating in on me ready to take a right-handed shot and the next thing I knew he had switched hands and he was shooting left-handed.

But Gordie wasn't the toughest player I ever faced; that would have to be Maurice "Rocket" Richard. I faced the Rocket in 1953 when I came up to the Rangers and he was the star of the Canadiens. From the blue line in, he was the best goal-scorer there ever was. He never used a slapshot but it was impossible to figure him out. He'd use a wrist shot or a backhander. You see, he was a left-handed shot playing right wing, so he would move the puck on his backhand a lot and just whip a backhander like you've never seen. And, remember, he used a completely flat-bladed stick in those days.

The amazing thing about Rocket was that he never scored in the same spot two shots in a row. He'd change all the time. He'd put one through your legs, then on the stick side up high and then low. Then, he'd put one on the glove side low and then high. He drove me up the wall the way he mixed his shots. When I saw Richard coming down the right wing, I would say a little prayer because he was the hardest to stop, bar none. I've often said that if I had to stop a penalty shot from Gordie and one from The Rocket, I'd have a better chance at stopping Howe.

How does Gordie compare with Wayne Gretzky?

Look at it this way; when Howe played in the NHL during his prime, it was a six-team league and competition never was any tougher. When Gretzky came in the league was loaded with expansion teams and getting bigger every few years. Sure, if Gretzky played during our era he would have gotten his share of goals but they would be in the vicinity of 50 or so, not like 70 or 80. But he would be right up there with the rest of the guys. The other thing is that Gordie was so physical whereas Gretzky is not. Wayne would have been run plenty playing against us and he wouldn't have had all the ice he has had and he wouldn't have gotten away with all the tricks that he did.

When I played, they coined the expression Goaltenders' Union just as a reminder that we puckstoppers are a special breed, although there never was such a union in reality. But we are different because of the position we play. We tended to be by ourselves and we were worrywarts. You've all heard about how Glenn Hall would vomit before every game. I know I was a worry wart and so was Gump Worsley.

I suffered when I let a puck go in. I felt responsible whether it was my fault or not. I would take it very seriously; so much so that I didn't even like anybody scoring on me in practice. When Punch Imlach coached me in Toronto, he would always say, "Practice is what you do in the games so you better work on your negative points in practice." And he was right.

Mostly, I stuck to my business, kept out of fights although I did get into trouble once and wound up with a ten-minute misconduct. We were playing the Rangers and Andy Bathgate, who was their star right wing, came dipsy-doodling down center and right in alone on me. By this time, I had developed a pretty good pokecheck for a goalie so I stuck out my stick at the last split-second and tried to jab the puck away from him. I missed the puck but Bathgate tripped as my stick accidentally went between his skates.

Andy went flying into the corner and the referee whistles me for a ten-minute misconduct — and also gives Bathgate a penalty shot! I really got perturbed about that, left my net and went after the referee, which I shouldn't have done.

This was just before Christmas and Andy came down the ice and put a neat deke on me and then slipped it into the net. As he went by, Bathgate shouted, "Bower, instead of having turkey for Christmas, you're going to eat crow!"

But I had the last laugh because we wound up beating them anyway. But that isn't the point; the point is I really didn't deserve the penalty because I never meant to let my stick go and trip him.

It was during my years with the Maple Leafs that the league began swinging over to a two-goalie system. Terry Sawchuk had come to Toronto and shared the goaltending with me. I saw that as competition and I wanted to remain number one. As a result, I played hurt a lot because I wanted to avoid sitting on the bench while Sawchuk took my place. If he got in, it could mean that I had to wait four, five or six games before I could get back between the pipes.

I thrived on work and never forgot what Imlach told me: "Johnny, the only way you're gonna stay up here is by working hard." And I did that. But I was always aware of Sawchuk and I'll tell you a little story about our competition. I was sitting out about the sixth game in a row and now the seventh game was coming up. I was getting a little rusty and wanted to play.

So, I got hold of one of my teammates, Eddie Shack, and said, "If you ever get a chance to fire a real good shot at Sawchuk in practice, do it." I knew that Terry would never try for them in the scrimmages. He was the worst practice goaltender I have ever seen. I mean, he would never try for them.

Sure enough, we're having a shooting drill and all of a sudden Shack comes in and fires at Sawchuk. I told him to shoot it on the ice and maybe he might get him in the ankle and bruise it a bit. Shack fired one on his glove side and accidentally broke Sawchuk's finger. I couldn't believe it. Well, I wound up playing ten straight games after that before Sawchuk got back. Ever since then I became real good friends with Eddie Shack.

The only goalie using a mask when I joined the Leafs was Jacques Plante of the Canadiens. He put one on in 1959, but nobody else did — at least not right away. We had to put up with some mighty hard shooters, including Bobby Hull, Dennis Hull and Boom Boom Geoffrion, but the difference was that none of them used curved sticks at the beginning. It wasn't until later that Hull, Mikita and Bathgate started with banana blades.

Frankly, I don't know how they can play with the curves on their sticks the way they do nowadays. They depend more on their shots than ever. On our Leaf team we had maybe three or four guys who could deliver a real hard slapshot. All the rest used the wrist shot. You don't see that much in the way of wrist shots anymore.

Most of the shots that hurt me, oddly enough, came in practices. The reason for that was that I eased up a little bit. I figured, "Oh, well, a guy's not going to shoot it up on me." The next thing I knew, I got the puck on the throat or got cut over the eye.

Which is not to say I didn't get hurt during the games. Over my career, I got between 250 and 280 stitches over the ice and Sawchuk had more than 300. His face was like a road map. I also had all my teeth knocked out and that hurt plenty. But, again, this was my livelihood and, for the most part, I stayed very, very alert. I knew that if I took my eye off the puck, I could lose an eye. Some goalies did. The Leafs once had a real good prospect in the 1940s named Baz Bastien. He took a puck in the eye, lost his sight in that eye and couldn't play in the NHL. Sure, I was scared, but I never showed it or anything because if you start thinking about it, you're going to play bad.

I played most of my big-league career for Punch Imlach, who was notorious as a taskmaster but that never bothered me. Punch never liked us to fool around in practice. We had scrimmages among ourselves that were as tough as the real games and, as a result, there were fights galore . . . Bobby Baun, Dickie Duff, Bob Pulford would get into bouts but Imlach didn't care. "After the workout," he'd say, "you can have your fun."

If you didn't play Imlach's way, man, oh, man, you were right back in the minors.

There was always someone breathing down your neck in Rochester waiting to take your job away. Of course, with Sawchuk alongside me, I didn't have to worry about motivation.

Terry and I used to sit next to each other in the dressing room and one day I said to him, "Terry, if I'm doing something wrong on the ice, would you please tell me?"

He looked at me and replied, "John, you're not doing anything wrong. You're doing just fine." But he wouldn't help me out or anything like that. He was strange in his own quiet way; a loner who didn't want to talk about goaltending or anything. He just wanted to go his own way and that was it.

Since I got no help from Sawchuk, I relied more and more on Imlach's advice. Punch had a good theory: whatever the players had to do during a practice, the goalie had to do as well. When they did stops and starts, I did them as well. If they worked on stickhandling, so did I. Punch believed that his goalies should be able to handle the puck and now we're seeing how the Ron Hextalls and Tom Barrassos are making that theory look good.

My specialty, aside from stopping the shots, was the pokecheck. I learned that trick way back when I came to the Rangers. Their great goalie, Chuck Rayner, was at the end of his career but he still was around Madison Square Garden and he was kind enough to take me aside. "Son," he said, "I want to help you out. I'm finished and now you have to learn how to play this position. One thing you have to learn is when to shoot the puck along the boards. You have to know when to dive for the puck when a guy comes close to you."

Rayner, who is in The Hockey Hall of Fame, was a terrific skater and puckhandler for his time. When he originally gave me the advice, I was skeptical. I said, "Well, the other goaltenders don't do that." He shot back, "Never mind the other goaltenders; I'm telling you what to do if you want to stay in the NHL. Just line up three or four pucks in front of the net about ten feet from the crease, move to the right and throw your body out; dive and then get up real quick and go for the next one. Get the four done, then line up the next four and keep doing it. And doing it and doing it, until you finally get it right."

It was good advice, and I took it and used it to perfect my pokechecking ability. But I also learned that you have to be aware of the oncoming forward giving you the fake and then going around you the way Gretzky likes to do it. They go around the net and bang it right in the other side. There were so many things I had to learn about goalkeeping. The funny thing was that as old as I was before I retired from the NHL, I always found something else to learn about.

A lot of rookies today can get away with not knowing all the tricks because they rely so much on reflexes. Felix Potvin of the Leafs is strictly a reflex goalie. He has the worst stance I have ever seen for a goalie, yet he stops the puck. He keeps his legs wide open and everything but he still stops them so you really can't change his style.

In some cases, it catches up with a kid. Remember Steve Penney who was a one-year sensation with the Canadiens back in the 1980s? They star for a limited amount of time and then their weaknesses catch up to them. Same with Peter Ing. Naturally, if you've got a good team in front of you — the way Ken Dryden did with the Canadiens in the late 1970s — you're going to last a long time because a goalie needs a lot of help from his defensemen and his forwards. If your defensemen aren't clearing rebounds, you're in a lot of trouble.

Still, lots of the goalie's help has to come from within himself. Self-motivation is very important. The coach can swear up and down at you, but if you don't want to do the job, you're not going to do it. I wanted to do it, you better believe that. I didn't have any superstitions the way other goalies did, but I was nervous and shaky and said a little prayer before the opening face-off. I stayed nervous until I stopped the first shot. After that, I calmed down. If I let the first one get by me, I started shaking a little bit.

On other occasions, I might stop 15 shots in the first period alone while the team did nothing for me, and yet Imlach would come into the dressing room and bawl me out.

But there was a method to his madness. The young guys would look at Punch and wonder, "Why is he bawling out Bower who saved us in that period?"

The reason was that Punch wanted them to say to themselves, "We have to pull up our socks and help our goalie." On that Toronto team there was only one guy who Punch always was very cautious about talking to, and that was our star left wing, Frank Mahovlich. For some reason, Punch and Frank couldn't get along and it might have been because Imlach realized that Mahovlich was a tremendous hockey player — when he wanted to be. Unfortunately, he didn't always seem to want it, and that's why the other teams would say, "Don't wake up The Big M else he'll get a hat trick on us."

Frank was a quiet guy and a good competitor but he was a little lackadaisical coming back [backchecking] for us. Imlach's feeling was that if you don't backcheck, you're going back to the minors, but Mahovlich was just too good for the minors.

I got along real well with Frank and I'd tell him that he was the greatest player in the world. Before some games, I'd say, "Frank, you can get a hat trick tonight." Then, he would go right out and score a couple of goals. But even when Mahovlich would score a goal or two or three, Punch would go right down the line on the bench and pat all the players — but he would go right past Frank. Why, I never knew, but that's the way Punch was.

Mahovlich almost wound up in Chicago. Arthur Wirtz, who owned the Blackhawks once wrote a check for a million dollars to buy Frank and the Leafs almost made the deal, but they reconsidered at the last minute and Frank stayed with us. He didn't get paid anything like the superstars do today but, then again, nobody did. We didn't get much money but we did have fun. We were very proud hockey players and, personally, I didn't care what Imlach offered me. Once, I tried to get a raise from Punch and he said to me straight out, "Do you like Toronto?" I said, "Yeah." So, he replied, "That's a hint; otherwise, you can go back to where you came from!" Which was the American League.

No, I wanted to stay in the NHL because I loved it. I really liked playing in Montreal best of all. The reason was that the Canadiens used to pump 30 to 40 shots at me and it's not often that that would happen. I liked that they kept me on my toes all the time because those Frenchmen could skate. They weren't called The Flying Frenchmen for nothing.

Oddly enough, I had my biggest problem playing in New York against my old team, the Rangers. You see, I wanted to beat them so badly after what they had done to me, and to show them they had made a mistake in trading me. So I tried extra hard in Madison Square Garden and, as a result, I played worse than ever. Meanwhile, the gang in the Garden balcony gave it to me pretty good but I shook it off just as any goaltender would.

But apart from New York, I did okay and the proof, I guess, is the length of time I stayed in the NHL and the Stanley Cups we won in Toronto. The better I got, the more attention the media paid to me. One of the big sources of interest was my age, because, when I came to the Leafs, I was up there in years compared to the other goalies. I always told the writers that I was born in 1924 [November 8] but they thought that I was older. They'd want to see my birth certificate, but I told them that I lost it in a fire, although I had never been involved in any kind of fire.

After we had won our last Stanley Cup in 1967, things began to slip and eventually my game began to falter as well. My eyesight began to go a little bit and Imlach finally said that I would have to go for an eye test. I was letting too many long shots get past me. My answer was, "Punch, it's not so much the long ones, it's a matter of me getting screened too much." By this time I was looking for excuses and Punch wasn't buying any of them. He'd say, "You're telling me you're screened and there wasn't a soul in front of you."

I came right back and said, "Punch, I'm tired of carrying the team on my back."

But I could read the handwriting on the wall, although it was hard for me to face up to it. Management finally said, "It's time that you hung up the pads for your own sake."

They promised me a job within the organization, which made me feel great. I accepted and became a scout for them. You see a lot of guys who retired and had another business to go to, but I didn't. Hockey was my life and I didn't know what else I was going to do.

I've been asked what enabled me to stay in professional hockey so long and the answer is simple: I did everything my coaches told me to do. Like Punch, he always harped on my having to play the angles and learning how to stop the puck and leave it for my defensemen. "Learn how to play your angles and work your butt off," he would say, "and you'll be in the NHL for a long time." That's why I was able to play for the Maple Leafs until I was almost 46 years old.

No goalie could stay that long in the NHL these days; not the way the game is played now, with the high-tech sticks, the high-speed of the shots and so many players able to shoot the puck so hard.

So, retirement didn't come hard for me. When I hung up my skates, I didn't want a special ceremony. But I would appreciate if, some day, the Maple Leafs retired my number one jersey. Teeder Kennedy, who was the great captain for Toronto teams in the 1940s and early in 1950, recently had his sweater retired. If they did that for me, it would make me feel good.

Not that I'm complaining, mind you. I'm still recognized, and when I go to a hockey rink, there always seems to be people who say, "Hi, Johnny, how are you?" I'm asked to sign autographs so, let's face it, I find it nice to be known. Parents turn to their kids and say, "There's Johnny Bower — he used to be goalie for the Toronto Maple Leafs."

I keep busy. I attend card shows, go to banquets and work for the United Way, trying to raise funds for Children's Wish, you name it.

Fans are always asking me questions about what it was like to play in the six-team NHL and how much fun we had in those days. Well, I can assure you that we had a lot of fun. The gang we had in Toronto really was a fun-loving bunch, even though Imlach was so tough. Always, you had to be careful about pranks. There was someone who would nail our shoes to the floor, tie our socks into knots and put wintergreen in our underpants.

But by far the most amusing story, I think, involved our dentures — that is, the false teeth. First of all, let me point out that the Maple Leafs had a policy that every player had to put his dentures in a little cup before he went out on the ice to play. You wouldn't play with false teeth in your mouth because if you ever got hit there, you could swallow the dentures and choke.

After the game, you'd take the false teeth out of the cup and put them back into your mouth. Same thing after a practice. On this particular day, Punch had scheduled a long practice because we had just lost a game so we all got out on the ice expecting a tough workout.

To our amazement, Imlach called it off in a very short time and nobody knew the reason why. Usually, in a situation like that, five or six guys would stay out on the ice with me to take some extra shots. This time, only one guy remained, which I thought was kind of strange, but I couldn't figure out why.

Anyway, he spent about five minutes shooting at me and then called it a day, so I did, too, and headed for the dressing room. When I got there, all the guys were waiting for me — which I also couldn't quite figure out — and they all had their heads down. When I saw that, I figured — uh, oh — something is wrong. I guessed that Punch had torn into the fellas because of the loss the night before.

Nobody said anything, so I sat down, as I always did, and put my hand in the little cup, took out the dentures and put them in my mouth. "Oh, my god! I said. They weren't my teeth. Somebody had exchanged them, and the first culprit who I thought of was Eddie Shack. "Where did you get these from?" I yelled at him. "You shouldn't do things like that."

But Shack so adamantly denied that he had done it that I was convinced it had to be someone else. Then, I realized who it had to be — our captain, George Armstrong, was always playing tricks on everybody. I confronted Army and he finally confessed and returned my teeth.

Meanwhile, I had taken the wrong teeth, which had been put in the cup, out of my mouth and looked at them. They seemed a bit strange to me, so I asked Armstrong, "Where did you get this plate?"

He couldn't keep himself from laughing. Finally, he said, "Johnny, I live behind a funeral parlor and my buddy, who works there, took them from a corpse and gave them to me."

Imagine how I felt now. And what a funny taste it left in my mouth!

That was only one of the pranks that had me as the victim. Another beauty was the Cigarette Butt Episode. It happened at a Sunday practice that Imlach had called at noon. The night before there had been a big rock 'n roll concert at Maple Leaf Gardens, and there still were cigarette butts all over the place.

I turned to Shack and said — as a joke — "Tell Punch that I was smoking a cigarette."

Eddie, always good for a laugh, said, "Hey, Punch, Bower is smoking a cigarette."

Punch turned to me and asked straight out whether that was true.

"Yeah," I answered, "I'm smoking a cigarette, all right."

Imlach ordered me into the dressing room and tore into me. "I'm running this hockey club," he barked, "and I have the last word around here and what the hell are you doing, smoking at practice!"

By this time, I realized that the joke had gotten way out of hand.

"Punch," I implored him, "I really didn't smoke."

"But Shack said you did."

"Honest, I didn't," I insisted.

Imlach practically had me on my knees denying it, but we had reached a point where I was so mad that I took off my equipment and went home. "There I go," I said to myself, "back to the American League."

After the practice, Armstrong drove over to my house and sat down with me. "John," he said, "you should have known better than to do that. Imlach was only trying to get you up for the next few games."

"Yeah," I told Army, "but there was no way he should have torn into me the way he did."

Anyhow, I slept it off and the next day, I returned to the Gardens and headed for the dressing room. There was Punch and he immediately looked at me and said, "So, you finally came to your senses. You're gonna put your pads on, eh?"

I apologized to Imlach that I had ever said anything and admitted my stupidity. Punch stared at me momentarily and finally said, "Get on the ice and start doing your warmups."

At that point I still wasn't certain where I stood with Punch until after the workout. He picked up a puck, skated over to me, stuck the rubber in my glove and said, "Here, you're playing tonight." Imlach was that type of guy.

When all was said and done, I have to say that I enjoyed playing for Punch — and with the rest of the guys on that Maple Leaf club. All in all, we were a happy family but, then again, when you're winning, everything goes great.

If I had the opportunity, would I do anything different? No, I wouldn't change anything, except for one thing. I would wear a mask — and a good, thick one, too. As Gump Worsley used to say about goaltending: You have only one head and you want to keep it!

-12-
Mike Palmateer

Mike Palmateer was not the best goalie ever to don the royal-blue-and-white of the Maple Leafs, but he was among the most colorful in the Toronto crease.

Although he never played for a Stanley Cup-winner, Palmateer goaled for the 1977-78 Leafs club that scored a memorable upset over the New York Islanders in a vicious seven-game series decided in sudden-death overtime.

Mike's Leafs eventually were eliminated by the Stanley Cup champion Montreal Canadiens but not without a battle. Palmateer's goaltending obtained rich critical acclaim and, for a time, he was regarded as one of the world's best netminders.

But the Leafs' fortunes soon were dissipated amid dissension and dismissals. Palmateer would, in time, find himself goaltending for the dismal Washington Capitals, despite injuries that would soon terminate his career.

Mike will never gain entrance to the Hockey Hall of Fame, but his exploits in the crease were both expert and eccentric. He tells about his goaltending exploits to Ontario-based reporter Wayne Geen.

Q: Where did you play all your minor hockey?

MP: I started out at age six like most kids and played house-league on Saturdays and Sundays in two different leagues. This is actually a good story in itself. I was a forward when I started out and won the scoring championship in both leagues.

In my third year, when I was eight, I started out as a forward, but a couple of months into the season, the coach said, "Who wants to be goalie for the practices?" I said, "I do," and he liked the way I played. The next game I started in net, and played well in the next couple of games. Before we knew it the other goalie got pissed off, quit and I became the goalie. At age nine, I was a goaltender, although I continued to play house-league hockey until I was 15. I won eight scoring championships in a row as a forward but didn't have the size to play at an advanced level.

Thanks to my scoring ability, I got my gambling instincts as a goalie to make all those neat saves when I was on my back. In those split seconds on the ice in the crease, I always pictured myself as a forward, thinking what I would do if I was in that position because I was a good goal-scorer. I could make quick judgment calls and make the great saves. They were last-ditch efforts.

Q: Did you ever wonder what would have happened if you had stayed on as forward?

MP: I only could have succeeded if my physique had changed for the bigger. Instead of playing at 165 lbs. I would have to have been 175 lbs. It was the Broad Street Bully days and big hockey was in. For me it had to be goalie or nothing.

Q: When you were growing up, did you have any favorite teams or players?

MP. I was a Leafs fan. Frank Mahovlich and Johnny Bower and all those guys were my childhood idols. It was natural because I wound up playing in Maple Leaf Gardens and wearing the blue and white of the Marlies. I moved all the way up through the Marlie system and won a Memorial Cup with the Marlies. My Marlies teammates were great. We won it in 1972-73. Then I was drafted by the Leafs, signed the contract — a two-way contract — and I figured this was great because they only had Wayne Thomas and Doug Favell in goal. I figured I'd knock those guys out in two seconds. Of course, I never even got a shot at training camp, and they had a third goalie, Gord McRae, who was playing for Oklahoma City, so they gave me the option of going to Oklahoma City. They said, "You might have to be the back-up and maybe not get a lot of action or you can go to Saginaw in the International League." That was still an affiliate of the Leafs but a step down league-wise. I opted to go where I could play, made my $20,000 and became the high-priced rookie on the team (*laughs*). I lasted there about four or five months and eventually got called up to Oklahoma City. I played the last half of my first year there, which was '74-'75, then played a full year there in '75-'76. In my third year, I started three or four games in Dallas before I was called up to the Leafs and, lo and behold, stayed.

Q: Do you remember your first game?

MP: We played in Detroit. I got the call around 11 p.m. or midnight the night before the game [in Dallas]. I hopped on a plane the next day and came up to Detroit, started, played well and we beat them 3-1. The move to bring me up was just a shake-up. It goes to show you what times were like: the Leafs had a couple of four-goal games against them, so they brought me in to wake up the club. As with any rookie goalie brought up, the game was like a Stanley Cup final for me. And I didn't give them an excuse to send me back down. I just played too well, so they had to keep me.

Q: Do you remember any stories? You did some oddball things, didn't you?

MP: One of the funny things that happened was in my second year with the Leafs. It was in training camp and I started the second half of a game. In those days, the trainers used to walk around with a tray of oranges between periods and I'd grab a handful and stick them in the top of my pad and eat them later through the game. I also was smoking at the time, and I was in the washroom having a cigarette between periods and stuck the smoking stuff in my equipment when it was my time to go out on the ice. So now the first save I make was against Dennis Hull of Chicago.

I make a great blocker stop and deflect the puck up into the crowd while my matches go flying on the ice. The referee picks up the matches. A minute later in a scramble, I'm down and I cover the puck. There are about three or four oranges laying on the ice. This just goes to show you how nervous I was — and excited.

Between that period and the third I went to the bathroom and forgot to do my suspenders up and played the third period with my ass hanging out of my pants.

Another one also involves Dennis Hull. Before my first game in Chicago, everyone was saying you've got to watch out for this play they do where Stan Mikita dumps it into the corner and as it comes off Dennis will come in and one-time the puck. They warned me that Hull always goes for the head — right to the top shelf. I mean everyone from Bower to [Jim] Gregory to guys on the team were saying watch out for Hull. They had me so psyched that when the play happened, just like that, Dennis one-timed it from about 25 feet out. I stood on my toes, but then he fanned on it and the puck went right along the ice and into the corner of the net. That's the first and last time ever in my life that I've ever "lifted" up on a puck.

Q: What do you think of Felix Potvin?

MP: I knew before the Leafs traded Grant [Fuhr] that Potvin could do the job. I knew they should trade Grant while they could and get something for him because I knew Felix could step in and do it and he has. He is a little different and a little unorthodox in style — not very aggressive for a goaltender.

Patrick Roy is a good one and I don't think there is any question that Fuhr was the best goalie in the last ten years; certainly one of the best of all time. I enjoy watching Grant play because he looks like he has a lot of fun.

Q: Do you still keep up on hockey? Do you watch a lot of hockey on TV?

MP: Not much at all. For years after I finished hockey, like a lot of professional athletes in a lot of sports, once they leave it they just want to leave it and I was like that. The last couple of years I've started to get into it; I'm becoming a fan again, as opposed to wishing I was there, getting those pangs and anxiety as opposed to watching a hockey game. But I still don't watch that much hockey, because I'm not involved in hockey. If I was involved in hockey or could get myself back into it, in a coaching position or a goalie position, then that's different. Then I'd bear down and watch.

Q: Would you like to coach?

MP: It all depends on where it is. I could help out a lot of the young guys. But at the same time, how can they replace my salary and the living that I'm making now? [Palmateer is a real estate agent for Re/Max Realty in Aurora, Ontario, 20 miles north of Toronto]. For me, it's been basically ten years since I've played and I'm established up here with a good job and two kids and some responsibility.

Q: What about your kids? Do they play hockey?

MP: No, I've got ballet dancers. I've got a seven-year-old girl and a two-year-old girl, and that's one of the reasons I'm not involved in hockey. If I had boys then I'd probably be coaching the kids and that sort of thing. On the bright side, there is no six o'clock in the morning at the hockey rinks. It's just four in the afternoon with ballet and gymnastics.

Q: Goalies salaries today . . . are they getting out of hand?

MP: I believe that whatever they can get, they deserve. I don't begrudge them or have any hard feelings that way. I'm like everyone else, I wish I was playing ten years later. But for me, what I had at the time was great. The great thing about it now is that you play six or seven years, get a good contract, and you're set for life, whereas when I played and went through my career, my goal was to try to get a house paid for, and to make the working part of my life easier.

It would have been nice to be a professional floater, a fisherman, and a golfer; I could do that. It's great to see the guys get the money. I think they deserve anything they can get.

But I can't believe it when these guys sign a contract for $700,000 and they've got four or five years left and the team just comes up and says "We'd like to give you another million a year." That blows me away. To me a contract is a contract, but anytime you can get more, go for it. I'm a firm believer in that.

Q: What was it like when Roger Neilson coached Toronto?

MP: We were like a seventh, eighth or ninth-place team; a pretty competitive team. We played a very defensive-oriented style of game, where I didn't have to worry about second, third or fourth rebounds like I did the last half of my career.

Q: Who were some of the other coaches you had?

MP: When I started off, Red Kelly was my coach for a year, then Roger coached me for a couple of years. He was definitely the best coach I ever had. I went through a bunch of coaches — Joe Crozier, [Punch] Imlach stepped behind the bench, Floyd Smith, Dan Maloney — a whole bunch of them.

Roger was called Captain Video, and he was ten years before his time. But he played us smart. He had good strategy. He didn't care about flash; he put a style that suited our hockey team at the time. I just thought he was great. He did a lot of little things that could make a hockey player better — things that you don't see — subtleties. He was definitely the best coach I ever had.

Q: What were your favorite places to play in the NHL?

MP: My best arena was Los Angeles; I always played well there. It had good lighting and that sort of thing. I also knew that my teammates — back then it was the only place in the sun — used to look forward to it as a place to relax. So I used to know if we had any chance of winning a game there that I'd better get some sleep and better stand on my head because we're not going to play that well. Of the 15 or 20 times we played there, I was a star in a dozen of them. I had a couple of bad games where they blew them by me, but all-in-all, that was my favorite rink. My worst rinks were Montreal, Quebec and Washington. All of those had the blue ice and I didn't like to play on blue ice because I found it harder to pick up the puck.

Q:　How come you played in Washington for two years?

MP:　They offered me the best money — in my worst rink! I don't regret that either. It was a good time in my life as far as the off-ice part of it goes. But I was hurt almost all the way through there. I was toast. I managed to play about 50 games or something that first year, but I know I only played about five of them healthy. The rest of them, they had me playing in tape, and broken this and torn that. I was just tape from head-to-toe. Still, I got eight assists and by Christmas I was about the fifth leading scorer on the team (*laughs*). We couldn't score very well on that team.

Q:　Washington was still relatively new, weren't they?

MP:　They'd been in it about six or seven years. The year that I left was the year they made great strides. They picked up about 14 players and they did that big Montreal trade getting [Brian] Engblom and [Rod] Langway. They really became a good team; I wish I could've been around for that one. Yet, when I look back I remember a great bunch of guys to play with and my defense, they tried every game. I loved them for that, but we just weren't very good. When I was getting my assists, they weren't deflecting off my blocker. I was nailing guys at center ice with breakaways.

Q:　Could Mike Palmateer play in the NHL today with his style of play? The floppy style he had?

MP:　Oh, sure. There is nothing wrong with the style I played. My style was best suited to a good team. I've got to admit that because I committed to the shooter. But no one ever came down the ice and blasted pucks by me, or seldom did I ever get scored upon on a breakaway. Ninety-five percent of the goals on me came from within ten feet of the net on deflections or rebounds or two-on-one passes and that sort of thing.

I believe in challenging. Let's face it, Felix Potvin has never stood up for a shot in his life. But he's taller and he's down and up and he never leaves his net. I could play a great game today — but it would take me another year to get ready for the next one. After 14 knee operations you can't bend too well.

Q: How do you feel about fighting?

MP: Fighting is part of the game. It always was when I was there. Fighting should be there, if two guys want to go at it. But I've never liked the goon tactics, like picking on the little guys, but to be honest, at the same time, at that level, it's not play fair, it's who wins. By whatever means it takes to win, you do that. And every edge you can take. That's why I said Roger Neilson is such a good coach — any little advantage he could go for, whatever small percentage, he'd take it. I did that as a goaltender. Anything you can get away with, do it.

Q: Don Cherry says do away with face shields.

MP: Kids come out of Junior and they're still going to have teeth. A lot of guys over the years have broken a cheekbone or just about lost an eye. The sticks are flying — you know, you're hooking and sticks are coming up under the arm. And I've seen guys lose their eyes that way. I don't think it is very sissy. Sissy is when you don't go in the corner or you step aside and not take a hit. That's a sissy! I believe they should wear helmets.

Q: Do you ever think back to when guys like Johnny Bower played and they didn't wear masks in net?

MP: It's hard to believe. It was a different game back then from what it is today. They didn't jam and crowd the net. They didn't shoot the puck nearly as hard; they had the straight sticks. It is a whole different game. When I played I got hit at least once in the face per game — not by pucks but by sticks. It depends on the style you play, too. I used to take a skate in the face every two or three games doing pokechecks. Johnny used to be the best there was at using a pokecheck. The only thing I did was I expanded on that and I not only went for the puck, but I used to play the feet. If the puck got by me I took the man out. I couldn't even imagine playing without a mask.

Q: What do you think of all the expansion?

MP: It's good for the game. I wish it was there when I was there. I
     could catch some sun, do some fishing, scuba diving between
     games — that would be great. It's good for the league as long
     as everyone is making money. It's more jobs, more hockey
     players out there.

Q: Are Europeans good for the game?

MP: Yes. They add a certain dimension, but you've got to question
     their intensity sometimes. But when it comes to talent,
     handling the puck, wrist shots, they always were better than
     we were in that regard. We play more of a bump-and-grind
     game and shoot from anywhere. But guys like Bure and
     Mogilny add another facet to the game.

     I can remember when I was in Saginaw and the Russians had
     an exhibition game against the Marlies, my old team. They
     brought me in to play the game. I had played a game the night
     before in Port Huron, drove all the way back to Saginaw on the
     bus, then got in my car and drove all the way to Toronto. I got
     to Toronto at seven o'clock in the morning after driving all
     night, went down to the rink for a practice, got about two hours
     sleep, played the game. I didn't play outstanding and we lost,
     7-6. We scored six goals on Vladislav Tretiak. It was pretty good
     but it seemed every time we got close, Kharlamov or Yakushev
     would go by four or five of our guys and pop it in the net.

Q: Did you ever play against Gretzky?

MP: Gretzky was one of those guys who you would never notice. I
     can remember a game at the Gardens that we lost 6-2 near the
     end of my career when we had the crappy team and Edmonton
     had the powerhouse. One goal he shot by me; two, he deked
     my defenseman so bad they took me out of the play — they
     took me right out of the net! At the end of the game, I didn't
     really notice him that much, but he had three goals and three
     assists. He was very subtle.

     Mike Bossy was a great shooter. He was the toughest guy in
     the slot. He didn't have to look at the net, just at the posts. His
     shots were always on the posts. He was as good as they come.
     He had half a dozen breakaways, and I don't think he ever
     scored on me on a breakaway. When he got the puck in the slot,
     with his quick shot, he was pretty good.

The goals against me always came from deflections and rebounds. I never got overpowered by shots or deked very much and breakaways were never a problem — just deflections and rebounds.

Q: Do you read books by ex-hockey players?

MP: I've been there; I've played the game. I don't care what John and Joe did ten years ago. I often wonder how much is real and how much is bullshit they're writing to make the story sound good. I stay away from that.

THE INCIDENTS

-13-

Alex Connell: THE GOALIE AND THE GANGSTERS

Hall-of-Famer Alex Connell rates as one of the all-time great goaltenders in the history of the National Hockey League. He holds the record for the longest shutout sequence, going six consecutive games without allowing a goal, an incredible feat he achieved in the 1927-28 season. He also shares the distinction, with Clint Benedict, of playing goal on Stanley Cup teams in two different cities. In 1926-27, Connell earned his first championship ring with the Montreal Canadiens. Perhaps the most well-known incident involving Connell occurred, however, when Connell came close to losing his life after getting involved with gangsters in New York City.

It was in 1932 at the old Madison Square Garden on Eighth Avenue and 50th Street in New York, and the Americans were hosting the Detroit Falcons in a game that would decide whether or not the Amerks would go into the playoffs later that spring. At the time, the Amerks were owned by the infamous Bill Dwyer, reputed mob boss, and undisputed King of the Bootleggers in New York as well as several other states.

The game was tied at the end of regulation time, 1-1, and the two teams went into a ten-minute overtime period. With about five minutes left in the period, Detroit received a penalty, giving the Amerks the much-needed advantage in manpower. New York players realized they had to take the initiative and win the game. It was a must situation.

The red, white and blue-clad Americans bore down and administered intense pressure on the Falcons. Red Dutton, then a battling defenseman for New York, took a blistering shot that, according to the goal judge, eluded Connell and ricocheted in —

and just as quickly out of — the net. The red light went on, and the Amerks celebrated their "win." But trouble was brewing — the referee, George Mallinson, disallowed the goal. He claimed he had a perfect view of the play and the puck never went in. Connell agreed.

"The shot might have looked like a score to the goal judge but the rubber definitely did not enter my net," recalled the erstwhile goalie.

During the melee that ensued, the goal judge berated the shocked goaltender with a string of the vilest profanity Connell had ever heard. Connell, being a man of dignity and pride, was not about to stand for any more of that kind of abuse. He skated around back of the net and, taking advantage of the man's nose which was sticking through the wire mesh, bopped the goal judge directly on his protruding proboscis. This sent the surprised and infuriated goal judge reeling in his own blood, and started a panic among the security force at the Garden who knew the man to be a "high official in Bill Dwyer's mob."

Alex Connell had unknowingly put his own life in grave danger with one well-placed, ill-timed punch. But Connell was more concerned with the game, and after play was resumed (the goal was not allowed) he held the Americans scoreless and the game ended in a 1-1 deadlock.

As Alex Connell left the ice, he noticed for the first time that there were policemen lining the walkway; everywhere he looked, he saw the boys in blue in great force blocking the spectators from approaching the players. When he got into the dressing room and began peeling off his sweaty uniform, two plainclothes detectives walked up, identified themselves to him, and then stood on either side of him, their guns drawn.

It was then that Connell realized the seriousness of the actions he had taken. It was explained to him that the man he had punched out was Dwyer's right-hand man, and that there might be some serious ramifications if proper precautions were not taken.

"Evidently," remembered Connell, "his finger on the red-light switch was as fast as the finger on his trigger."

After he had finished dressing, Connell was quickly shuffled into a waiting taxi and driven, along with his police escort, to the hotel where the team was staying. The cops combed the lobby for suspicious-looking characters before bringing in the befuddled Alex Connell. He was then given strict instructions not to leave his room for the remainder of the evening, and that he would probably be quite safe if he followed those words of caution without question. Needless to say, Connell was willing to obey, his fear and anxiety mounting with every cloak-and-dagger maneuver by the detectives.

Connell recalls how the rest of the evening went: "An old friend was visiting with me that night and after we had talked about the strange goings-on, we decided to leave the hotel and get some sandwiches before I went to bed.

"We went out the front door and had only walked about ten feet when I remembered the cop's warning. Then I noticed there were some people standing around us. One big, mean-looking guy looked right at me and came toward us. We ducked into a diner and seated ourselves at separate counters. The large man came in and ordered me to go over to him for questioning. I paid no attention to him, so he repeated his order, adding that if I knew what was good for me I'd do what I was told.

"Then I walked over to him. He demanded, 'Aren't you Alex Connell, goalkeeper with the Detroit Falcons?' I replied that not only did I not know who Alex Connell was, but that I'd never heard of any Detroit Falcons.

"After a couple of minutes of him repeating the question and me repeating my answer, he apologized for bothering me and left."

When the cops heard about the incident from the hotel night manager, they decided to stand guard outside Connell's room for the rest of the night.

The next day Connell learned that his quick thinking and fast talking had probably saved him from a "one-way ride" with the gunslinging hoodlums.

"Years later a New York newspaper man told me that the police had established the fact that both of the gangsters I encountered that night had come to sudden endings. When I asked how, he said, 'Bang! Bang!'"

-14-
KING AND "COWBOY"

Eddie "Cowboy" Convey was a journeyman forward who had been longtime friends with King Clancy, then starring for Toronto. Convey was barely hanging in there with the New York Americans.

When Convey came in with the New York sextet, word spread around the Maple Leafs dressing room that Cowboy was on the brink of demotion to the minors. This concerned the sensitive Clancy, who told his Toronto colleagues that something had to be done for Convey. "Look," King said, "if we get a few goals up, let's make it easy for Cowboy and help him score a couple."

Sure enough, the Leafs sped to a 4-0 lead and had the game well in hand when Convey skated onto the ice against Toronto's Kid Line with Clancy on defense and Lorne Chabot in goal. King winked at Conacher to be sure that Charlie got the message, and in the next moment Convey skated past Conacher, who was kind enough not to check him. Cowboy was one-on-one with Clancy, and King fell backwards on his skates, allowing Convey to break in on the goaltender.

Chabot was aware of Convey's scoring drought, and he believed that his best move to allow Cowboy to score was to make no move at all. He simply remained inert in the nets as Convey sized up the situation. There was plenty of air to the left and plenty to the right. Cowboy had a delectable choice, and he promptly fired the puck considerably wide of the target — and so high that it flew directly into the grandstand.

Uncertain whether to be furious or amused with Convey, the Leafs eventually returned to the bench and agreed that their former teammate deserved one more chance. The same group of Toronto players was on the ice a few minutes later when Cowboy galloped toward Chabot.

In what amounted to an almost precision maneuver, Conacher permitted Convey to pass him, and Clancy artfully faked a body-check that missed. "Eddie went cruising in on Chabot," Clancy remembered, "who was ready to step aside and, in fact, fell to the ice, giving Convey a whole goal to shoot at. Bam! Eddie shot the puck, and don't you think he hit Chabot right in the Adam's apple with the darn puck. Chabot went down, choking and gagging."

For a change, the Leafs stopped worrying about Convey and rushed to their injured goaltender. Chabot looked up and snapped, "Cut this nonsense out or that guy will kill me!" It was then that Clancy realized his altruism had gone too far. He looked at Conacher, perhaps thinking that one more try might be in order, when Conacher stared back at King and shouted: "Screw Convey!"

Thus, Chabot was saved from another throat injury.

-15-
THE VETERAN AND THE ROOKIE

Bill Durnan of the Montreal Canadiens won his first Vezina Trophy in 1944 and, according to his coach Dick Irvin, it was one of the worst things that ever happened to the Hall-of-Fame goaltender. "From that time on," Irvin asserted, "Durnan became a man possessed. Winning the Vezina became an obsession with him."

That obsession resulted in Durnan winning the goaltenders' prize a total of six times, concluding with the 1949-50 season when an extraordinary event took place.

Durnan, although as great as ever, was getting on in years, and the Canadiens owned a splendid youngster named Gerry McNeil, who played for their Montreal Royals farm team in the Quebec Senior Hockey League. If Durnan was ever injured, McNeil was on hand as a replacement.

One night, Durnan was involved in a serious accident which Irvin believed shortened his career. "A skate pierced his head," said Irvin, "and wrecked his nervous system. He cracked up after that."

Actually, McNeil replaced Durnan for only six games out of the 70-game schedule and turned in a magnificent 1.50 goals-against average. Durnan's mark after 64 games was 2.20. Together, they compiled a 2.14 average to win the Vezina.

"Durnan was so obsessed with the Vezina," said Irvin "that if he had lost it that year he played (1949-50), I think he would have been back playing goal the next year, bad nerves and all."

When the 1950 playoffs began, Durnan was in the Montreal net facing the New York Rangers. He played three games and allowed 10 goals for a 3.33 goals-against average and, clearly, was not his championship self. As a result the Rangers, who had been underdogs, took a surprising lead in the series. Irvin, who was coaching Montreal at the time, decided to yank the veteran Durnan and gamble with the rookie McNeil.

"I'll never forget the night Durnan gave way to McNeil," Irvin recalled. "Gerry was as nervous as a kitten, so I thought if I got Bill to take him into another room and talk to him, the kid would quiet down."

Irvin made the suggestion and the two netminders — the grand old man and the heir to the throne — disappeared into the anteroom. After a reasonable period of time Irvin expected them to come out so that McNeil could get on with the match, but neither was to be seen.

"Dick decided to investigate," a hockey writer remembered, "and went into the room. There he found his two goalies sitting together, crying!"

Durnan was sobbing: "Don't worry about a thing, Gerry. Everything is going to be all right."

In the other corner sat McNeil. Author Ed Fitkin recalled: "Gerry said nothing; he was just sobbing." Irvin was dumbfounded — momentarily.

"I thought I pulled a boner," said Irvin, "but that night McNeil played one of the greatest games of his life!"

-16-

"Pop" Kenesky: THE MAN WHO MADE EVERY SAVE IN THE NHL

For almost 70 years, each time a goaltender extended a padded leg to kick away a potential opposition tally, one man was responsible. Emil "Pop" Kenesky, once a mild-mannered Hamilton, Ontario harness maker, stitched together every leg pad worn by a professional goalie — every one through the six-team NHL era.

Before his death, every day since 1916, Pop climbed the 19 worn steps to the loft above his sporting goods store. When he bought the store with a down payment of $15, he planned to use his $5 sewing machine to make harnesses and saddles. Pop learned his trade in the hamlet of St. Jacobs, near Kitchener, where his parents settled after immigrating from Germany.

He got the idea for going into the goaltending pad business in 1926, when he went to a senior Catholic League hockey game and noticed the short width of the cricket pads worn by the Hamilton goalie. "Why don't you make them so they stick out at the sides?" Pop suggested. "There's nothin' to cover it in the rules."

Pop brought the cricket pads back to his loft and extended the width to 12 inches. Soon, the Kenesky pads were the rage of the league, and Hamilton's professional hockey team, the Tigers, heard of Pop's invention. When the Tigers lost their first eight games, the coach decided a radical change might help netminder Jake Forbes, so he had Pop design new pads for his goalie. With Jake wearing Kenesky pads, Hamilton won the very next game.

"His old pads weighed 17 pounds," Pop recalled. "I made him some that weighed only seven pounds together. They started callin' him Jumpin' Jakie. He could almost jump over the net, he was so light."

At age 96, Pop was still turning out his patented product at the rate of about 300 a year. He never could figure out the "goldarn" manufacturing business, nor did he ever teach anyone else how to make his pads. He was content to let his three sons run the shop downstairs while he stitched away the days in his loft.

Pop adjusted to the change in times. "I'd stuff 'em harder than I did years ago," the little old fellow would say. "Now they weigh from 11 to 14 pounds a pair — since they started that goldarn slapshot."

Pop stood just 5'6", 135 pounds, and age and hard work had gnarled his powerful hands, but goalies swore by his pads and sought him out even in emergency situations.

"One morning a fella come in here and says, 'I'm Sawchuk,'" Pop remembered. "He'd been traded from Detroit to Boston. But Detroit wouldn't let him take his pads with him. He needed a pair for that night for a game in Toronto. Well, sir, we got to work and delivered them in Toronto before the game started. I guess that was the last game I saw."

The most expensive pair of Kenesky pads went for $135, a long way from the $12.50 he once charged goaltenders in the 1930s, but still not inflationary by today's standards. The process, however, was much the same over the years: he used three pieces of cream-colored horse-hide, felt, and rubberized canvas, then stuffed the front with kapok and the sides with deer hair.

Wilf Cude (Toronto Maple Leafs) and Harry Lumley (Detroit Red Wings) were two of the more inventive goalies who came up with lasting changes to Kenesky's original design. Cude asked Pop to make him pads in which the rope-filled outside extended over the knee, a style which many goalies adopted. Lumley discovered the "scoop," a pocket in the shin area which causes the puck to drop to the ice on impact, rather than boomeranging out to another attacker.

Other goalies' attempts at improving Pop's pads were not as successful. "Once, a fella named Harvey Teno in the American League said to me, 'Hey, Kenesky, you're puttin' too much paddin' inside of your legs.' I tried to tell him he needed it there. But I made 'em the way he wanted.

"Well, he got hit there," Pop said, always spitting tobacco juice as he spoke, "and I'll be goldarned if he didn't quit hockey."

Earl Robertson of the old New York Americans may have come up with the strangest addition to the Kenesky pads. He insisted that a rabbit's foot be added to the stuffing in each pad. Pop, as usual, bowed to the goalie's request.

In later years, orders for pads began arriving from all over the world. "I've sent them to England, Switzerland . . . all over," Pop once said.

One satisfied customer was a young Swedish goalie, Christer Sehlstedt, who was so happy when his pads arrived, he immediately put pen to paper to thank Pop and commend his craftsmanship. "My pads have just arrived," wrote Sehlstedt. "They look superb. They are almost ready for action when they arrive from you. They are so easy to break in."

Christer and many other goalies who have reaped the benefits of Pop's talent would be surprised to see the small quarters where Kenesky once practiced his trade. The ingredients for the goalpads were usually flung about the room in disarray, while finished pads lined the walls and shelves of his two tiny rooms, each containing a bare lightbulb and a single window. His machine was electric, and its markings read "International Harness Machine Co., Cincinnati, O."

"I was the first guy to run that thing," he said. "Then I bought it for five dollars. Got to make the parts for it myself. Don't know if that company is still in business."

When Pop was in business, he didn't get too many repeat orders, though not because he had any dissatisfied customers. Kenesky pads were known for their longevity. He could proudly point to a pair of goalpads sent for repairs from Preston that were 35 years old.

When asked about retirement, the old man would be puzzled. After over 90 years of drinking, smoking, chewing and working most of his waking hours, retirement was always far from the feisty old guy's mind.

"Retire?" he would echo. "I'll retire when I get old and the goaltenders stop coming in." Pop never did retire and the goaltenders never stopped coming in. The old man himself was still stitching pads together until his death at age 96.

-17-
A GOALTENDER'S LIFE IS . . .

It has been said, with some justification, that a young man has to be at least slightly crazy to pursue a career as a goaltender. The reasons are obvious. The goaltender stands in front of a net six feet wide by four feet high and attempts to prevent a six-ounce piece of hard vulcanized rubber from flying past him. What makes this an exceptionally difficult operation is that the puck often flies at speeds of more than 100 miles per hour, making it practically invisible to the goalie.

Many contemporary hockey people are inclined to believe that the present-day fire-wagon brand of hockey is fraught with more problems for a goaltender than the slower-paced game of yesteryear. Old-timers such as Johnny Gottselig, who played for the Blackhawks in the 1930s, would not necessarily agree. Gottselig remembers goaltender Charlie Gardiner's death in 1934, two months after the Hawks won their first Stanley Cup. "Chuck was in his prime when he died," said Gottselig. "It was only his sixth season in the league. I think his whole life was shortened by goaltending. He was always alone . . . Goalies are probably the loneliest guys in the world."

Not every goaltender who entered the National Hockey League has been a solitary introvert. The Maple Leafs' Turk Broda was a gregarious, fun-loving type who enjoyed a joke as much as the next fellow, although quite often the joke was on him.

Turk was first scouted by the Detroit Red Wings and invited to their training camp in the 1934-35 season. "He still had hay behind his ears," said veteran Lorne Duguid, "and he was an inviting target for dressing-room fun." What made Broda such an obvious target was his raucous blue serge suit with white stripes, which made him look like a zebra.

Unknown to Broda, the Red Wings' activities were closely followed that season by a tailor who happened to be a fanatic hockey fan. The tailor showed up for Detroit scrimmages and occasionally did some work for the players. One afternoon, while Broda was on the ice practicing, the tailor arrived in the Red Wings dressing room and asked Duguid if there was any work to be done.

Thinking fast — not to mention sadistically — Duguid walked over to Broda's locker and picked up Turk's blue serge suit. With a straight face, Duguid advised the tailor that he had bought the suit and to his dismay discovered that the pants were much too long. "Do me a favor?" Duguid asked. "Shorten these about ten inches and bring them back within the hour because I have a date tonight."

The obliging tailor went to work on the pants and completed the operation long before Broda ended his workout. "As he climbed into his trousers," recalled Vern DeGeer, then the *Montreal Gazette's* columnist, "Broda let out a scream of anguish. The tailor had shortened them so that the cuffs ended halfway between his ankles and his knees."

Desperate to conceal his embarrassing appearance, Broda loosened his suspenders hoping to lengthen the pants. But that only succeeded in dropping the waistline down around his hips, which was as offensive looking as the short trouser legs. "He was like an old-fashioned gal in hobble skirts," said DeGeer.

Duguid looked on with an expression of sympathy on his face. He had thought that the tailor would merely tuck the extra material up the underside of the pants. But on closer inspection Duguid discovered that he had actually cut off the material, leaving Broda no opportunity for readjustment.

"It was the most expensive gag I ever pulled," Duguid admitted. "I suddenly realized it was the only suit of clothes Turk had. So I had to loan him a pair of my trousers, and then take him downtown and buy him a new suit."

When Broda enlisted in the Canadian Army in 1943, during World War II, he was succeeded by a tall, gaunt-looking young man named Frank McCool. A scholarly type, McCool eventually left hockey to become a journalist. By 1954 he had become the sports editor of the *Calgary Albertan*, which seemed to justify his decision to quit goaltending at a relatively early age.

"I quit early," said McCool, "mainly because of ulcers. Why I had ulcers I don't know, but it didn't help being a goalie. It's the toughest, most unappreciated job in sports. The goalie always takes the rap. It's always his fault when you lose. The crowd gets on you and then the papers pick it up. Soon the players themselves begin to think you're to blame."

For McCool, the strain was mental. For other goaltenders, the physical punishment can tire them and inspire them to hang up their pads. One of the first of the really great goalies to succumb to exhaustion was Clint "Benny" Benedict, who broke in as a pro in 1913 with the Ottawa Senators. "After the first couple of seasons," said Benedict, "I lost count of the stitches they had put in my head. They didn't have a goal crease in those days and the forwards would come roaring right in and bang you as hard as they could. If they knocked you down, you were supposed to get back on your feet before you could stop the puck. Those were the rules."

A strapping six-footer, Benedict absorbed terrific punishment for 18 years. Obviously his sturdy physique was an asset to his playing longevity. "I remember," he once said, "at least four times being carried into the dressing room to get all stitched up and then going back in to play. There were some other times, too, but I don't remember them."

Benedict ranked with Georges Vezina, George Hainsworth and others of the early great goaltenders. He played on five Stanley Cup champion teams, four of them in Ottawa, and appeared in 32 Stanley Cup games. But one of his signal contributions to the art of goaltending was his innovative decision to fall to the ice in order to block a shot. Until Benedict came along, it had been traditional for goaltenders to remain upright throughout the game.

"It actually was against the rules to fall to the ice," Benny explained. "But if you made it look like an accident you could get away without a penalty. I got pretty good at it and soon all the other goalies were doing the same thing. I guess you could say we all got pretty good at it until about 1914, and the next season the league had to change the rule."

Benedict's revolutionary maneuver was greeted with the same hostility as Jacques Plante's decision to wander out of his net when he joined the Montreal Canadiens in the '50s. The first time Benedict displayed his flopping style in Toronto, the fans shouted, "Bring your bed, Benny!"

There are those who say that Benedict single-handedly won the 1923 edition of the Stanley Cup for Ottawa. The Senators were playing Vancouver for the title, and in the final game of the series Ottawa was nursing a 2-1 lead with only three minutes remaining in the contest.

At this point the Senators were penalized twice in succession and had to defend against the determined Vancouver club with only three skaters to the home team's five. It was Benedict who now rose to the challenge and blunted every one of the enemy's dangerous thrusts. "We were out on our feet at the end," Clint said, "but we won."

Significantly, it was not long afterward that New York Rangers manager Lester Patrick defined the importance of a goaltender to a hockey club. "The goalie," said Patrick, "is 70 percent of a team's strength. A good one can make a weak team awfully tough to beat. A mediocre one will ruin his team."

Ironically, Patrick later was to feel personally the truth of his analysis. For during World War II the Rangers had a mediocre team and some of the worst goaltenders hockey has seen. One of them was Ken McAuley, who was in the nets one night against the Red Wings and lost the game, 15-0, a record that still stands.

Two decades later the Rangers were to exact sweet revenge against the Red Wings for that shellacking in a strange episode at Madison Square Garden. It was late March, 1962, and the Rangers and Red Wings were neck and neck in a race for the fourth and final playoff berth. Each team had 57 points for the season, and the two points that would go to the winner of the upcoming game would just about clinch fourth place, which would be the final playoff berth.

It promised to be an extraordinary game for many reasons. Doug Harvey, the Rangers rookie coach, was also taking a regular turn on defense and, despite his advanced age, was playing like an all-star. What's more, the usually downtrodden Rangers were making one of their rare bids for a playoff position. New York's captain, Andy Bathgate, led the league in scoring with a small margin over Bobby Hull of the Chicago Blackhawks, and Gordie Howe, the immense Detroit right wing, was aiming for his 500th NHL goal.

The game that developed into one of the most exciting ever played on Madison Square Garden ice started with the stickhandling magic of Bathgate, who sidestepped his way around the Red Wing defense and scored on a 15-foot shot that Detroit goalie Hank Bassen failed to handle. But before the first period ended, Howe skimmed a pass to line mate Claude Laforge, who beat Ranger goalie Lorne "Gump" Worsley.

With the score tied 1-1 in the second period, Howe took command. The Red Wings were short one man (Laforge was in the penalty box) when Howe captured the puck at center ice and loped toward the Ranger zone. "Only one defender stood in his path," said Ken Rudeen of *Sports Illustrated*, "and that man was Harvey, the greatest defenseman in hockey."

Howe has always had the extraordinary knack of appearing to be doing nothing very much at the precise moment he is executing an extremely intricate maneuver. This time he innocently approached the waiting Harvey and moved calmly to the right. Suddenly Howe jerked his body to the left in an apparent drive for the other side of Harvey. But it was only the old pro's feint. Interpreting the move a split second too late, Harvey tried to thwart Howe with a thrust of his extended hip. He did manage to graze the onrushing Red Wing, but not hard enough to drop Howe to the ice. Gordie regained his equilibrium and, with his stick and puck to the right of his body, moved in on the crouching Worsley.

Quite properly, the goalie expected a backhand shot — except that Howe was the only player in the league who could shoot ambidextrously, and Gordie quickly switched hands, moving the puck and stick to his left. Before the goaltender could move, Howe had shot the puck past him for his 500th goal and a 2-1 lead for Detroit.

The Rangers weren't about to capitulate, Howe or no Howe. Before the second period ended, they tied the score, 2-2, thus setting the stage for one of the most freakish episodes in hockey. It developed late in the third period with the teams still in the death grip of a deadlock match and no break in sight.

With the red-headed Bassen playing one of his better games at the Detroit goal cage, the Rangers launched a particularly threatening attack. Bathgate and his longtime sidekick, Dean Prentice, moved over the Detroit blue line as the Red Wing defense slipped out of position. Prentice caressed the puck on his stick along the left side of the ice, but appeared to have no better than a five-to-one chance of beating Bassen from this relatively difficult angle.

However, Bassen had a reputation for impetuous moves. He often left the goal crease to engage in fights and was notorious for wandering far out of the net after stray pucks. This, however, was no time for playing around.

For reasons known best to himself, Bassen skated ten feet forward and confronted Prentice head on. At the moment it seemed to be a brilliant riposte, for the Ranger was forced farther and farther from the net. Then the unbelievable happened.

Bassen's stick left his right hand, slid across the ice, hit the black-taped blade of Prentice's stick, knocked the puck harmlessly into the corner of the rink, and sent Prentice crashing into the boards. For most onlookers it was difficult to determine whether Bassen had panicked, had deliberately planned to release his stick, or had accidentally let it slip out of his thick leather gauntlet. Certainly it would be an enormously difficult call for a referee. But the rule book clearly states that the fouled player in such a situation should be awarded a penalty shot, which amounts to a clear, unimpeded play on the goalkeeper. The referee blew his whistle and, to the complete dismay of the Red Wings, ordered that a penalty shot be awarded.

This, in and of itself, was a rarity. There had not been a penalty shot called at Madison Square Garden for six years, and only nine had been called in the league throughout the 1961-62 season. But there was no mistaking the fact that Prentice had been fouled and had the right to take the prize.

At this point still another extraordinary thing happened. The referee designated Bathgate as the man to take the shot. This might have been legal had Prentice been disabled on the play, but Dean was fully recovered from his crash into the boards and joined his teammates on the sidelines as Bathgate accepted the puck in preparation for his one-on-one foray against Bassen.

The play would be worth $100,000 to the Rangers, and as much as $300,000 in total prize money if they went on to win the Stanley Cup. "To the crowd," said Rudeen, "it was like watching the clash between cobra and mongoose. The broad expanse of white ice was empty except for the two opposing players. The crowd hushed. The referee blew his whistle."

One of the most perceptive players in the league, Bathgate was well aware of Bassen's strengths and weaknesses. He was particularly conscious of the goalie's impulsiveness, so Bathgate decided to take advantage of that flaw in Bassen's style. At center ice the Ranger captain carefully pushed the puck ahead of him, seemingly in slow motion. Gradually he picked up speed as he passed over the Detroit blue line, one eye on the puck, the other studying Bassen for the crucial move that would suggest the goaltender's strategy.

Bassen did precisely what Bathgate had hoped he would do — the goalie moved forward out of his crease, leaving enough room for the Rangers ace to toy with his foe. Bathgate's first ploy was a drop of his shoulder, suggesting a move to the right side of the net. The Detroiter fell for the trick so easily that it appeared he was being pulled away from the goal by invisible strings. While Bassen was falling hopelessly into Bathgate's trap, the Ranger casually moved to his left and backhanded the puck into the yawning net.

The controversial goal gave the Rangers the game and fourth place. Yet to this day Bassen and the Red Wings could rightfully claim that they were the victims of the referee's mistake, for it was Prentice and not Bathgate who should have taken the penalty shot.

"The ref gave New York the game on a wrong call," said Detroit coach Sid Abel. The Rangers later agreed with Abel, but they weren't about to relinquish their opportunity to gain entrance to the playoffs. The gloating New Yorkers were soon to get their comeuppance, however, in strange quirk of irony in the playoffs. Once again, a wrong call by the referee thwarted a team's chances for victory.

Underdogs in the semi-final round against the second-place Toronto Maple Leafs, the Rangers lost the first two games at Toronto, but then returned to the friendly confines of Madison Square Garden and stunned the visitors with 5-4 and 4-2 victories. With regained momentum, the New Yorkers returned to Toronto for the pivotal fifth game of the best-of-seven series.

The game, played on April 5, 1962 at Maple Leaf Gardens, was a marvelous display of hockey. After three periods of regulation time, the evenly matched clubs were tied 2-2. One period of sudden-death overtime failed to bring about a decision, which meant another session of pulsating sudden death. It was the Rangers who opened the attack and seemed on the verge of beating ancient Johnny Bower in the Toronto goal. But the New York shots fell short, and the Leafs regrouped and counterattacked shortly after the four-minute mark.

Gump Worsley, who had played competently throughout the series for New York, was tested on a long shot. He stopped the drive, but somehow lost the puck as it fell behind him — directly in front of, but not over, the goal line. Worsley fell backward, like a man in the act of fainting, and landed on top of the puck.

Having thwarted the drive, Worsley remained horizontal awaiting the referee's whistle to signal the end of play. One second, two seconds, three seconds elapsed, and still no whistle. Nevertheless, Worsley was convinced that enough time had passed to earn a stoppage of play, so he lifted his head off the rather uncomfortable puck-pillow and prepared to rise for the ensuing face-off.

The face-off never came.

The referee had lost track of the puck momentarily and by mistake delayed blowing his whistle. At exactly the moment that Worsley lifted his head, Toronto center Red Kelly skated across the mouth of the goal, saw the unguarded puck big as life, and quickly pushed it into the cage. The red light flashed on and the Maple Leafs won the game, 3-2. On their long trip back to New York, the defeated players were heard to echo the same remark made by the Red Wings only weeks earlier: "The blankety-blank referee made a wrong call."

Stunned by the setback, the Rangers lost the sixth game of the series, 7-1, and were eliminated from the playoffs.

Worsley, the unfortunate victim, was to be plagued by misfortune throughout his long and colorful career. As much as anyone, the Gump symbolized the beleaguered goaltender who, like Buster Keaton in the movies, fought on despite misfortune. But Worsley really was unique in his profession. He had an obsessive fear of flying. The problem began to plague Worsley when he was a 19-year-old playing for the New York Rovers, a minor-league farm team of the Rangers. The Rovers were flying east after a game in Milwaukee when flames began spouting from one of the engines on the plane. It was touch and go for about a half-hour as the pilot sought to control the blaze and find a suitable place to land. He finally accomplished both and the aircraft touched down in Pittsburgh.

Physically, Worsley emerged from the plane unharmed. But the traumatic experience of seeing an engine enveloped in flames at 20,000 feet is not something that's easily forgotten.

And Gump didn't forget.

Throughout his long and successful NHL career, he worried

more about the takeoff of Boeing 707s than he did about the takeoff of those black rubber pucks that flew in his face.

Somehow Worsley managed to cope with the strain until 1967, when the league expanded to 12 teams and he was compelled to fly from coast to coast as his team, the Montreal Canadiens, fulfilled their schedule. Then, in the 1968-69 season, it finally happened. Happy-go-lucky Gump Worsley cracked under the strain.

He was en route to Chicago when he leaned over to his seat companion, trainer Larry Aubut, and whispered, "Get Big John!"

"Big John" was Jean Beliveau, the team captain. He listened to Worsley and counseled, "Wait 'til we get to Chicago. Then we'll see what happens."

But the Gump had made up his mind — he was going to quit. As soon as the team landed in Chicago, he phoned his wife and the Canadiens manager, Sam Pollock, and told them he had had it. No more flying, no more playing. Pollock patiently listened and suggested that Worsley return home. A week later Gump was working with a Montreal psychiatrist, trying to understand and cope with his fear of flying.

"We talked a lot," said Worsley. "He tried to work me through it. He helped a lot. At first, I just took it easy. My wife and I started to go to the odd game when the club was at home. Then I started skating again all alone, and finally I put on the pads. Pretty soon I felt not bad."

Worsley managed to recover enough of his aplomb to return to the Montreal lineup as the Canadiens entered the homestretch of the 1968-68 campaign. The Flying Frenchmen finished in first place in the East Division and went on to win the Stanley Cup, and Worsley played a key role in the triumph. As for the plane trips, well, he reached a degree of resignation over that problem. "I know I have to fly," Worsley said. "It's part of the game now. On charters it's not so bad. I spend my time in the cockpit. It feels different up there because the pilot explains things and you can see what's going on."

The Canadiens signed the Gump to another contract in 1969-70, for they believed that he had licked his flying phobia. And he had. But midway in the season the Gump once again left the team. This time, it was another phobia — practice phobia. Management said Worsley was out of shape. Manager Pollock suggested that Gump spend a few weeks trimming off his fat in the minors. Worsley refused and, after a clash with coach Claude Ruel, he was suspended from the team.

Later, Worsley, who had been a chief cog in the first-place Canadiens' machine a year earlier, was traded to Minnesota, a club that had gone 20 games without a win. But the moment the beleaguered Worsley arrived in Minneapolis, the North Stars regrouped, regained their equilibrium and, with the pudgy, airsick, and out-of-shape Worsley leading the way, marched to a playoff berth. Such an ironic twist of fate suited the colorful goaltender's sense of humor perfectly.

For the netminders who happened to play for the Boston Bruins during their drought years of the '50s, goaltending was not particularly enjoyable, either. During one period of extreme bombardment of the Bruins cage, the Boston management could have been forgiven if it had taken out a life insurance policy for every goaltender who put on a Bruins uniform.

Roger Barry, the hockey writer for the Quincy, Massachusetts *Patriot-Ledger*, was so moved by the Beantown blitz that he wrote an article about the "discovery" of the perfect Bruin goalie. The man's name was something like Pierre Lafong and he purportedly was discovered in the wilds of northern Quebec. What made Pierre so ideal for the position, said Barry, was that he measured almost a perfect five by five — five feet tall and five feet wide — thereby blocking all but a few inches of the goal area. In order to put the puck past him, the opposition would require a derrick or a blowtorch.

Publication of the "Perfect Pierre" story in the Boston Garden hockey program caused a tidal wave of excitement around the league over this truly amazing find. Bruins fans were delirious with joy and opponents wondered with consternation just how they would cope with this Chinese Wall of a goalie.

Barry was somewhat startled by the reaction. "It was only a gag," he said. "Mr. Five-by-Five was merely a product of my imagination, not the Bruins farm system." But the beleaguered Boston hockey fans, who were prepared to cling to any thread of hope about their team, accepted the myth of "Mr. Five-by-Five" and, at least temporarily, converted it into their own form of reality.

-18-
THE GOALIE WHO SCORED A GOAL

Ever since R.F. Smith drew up the first rules for hockey in the late 1800s, it had been generally accepted that a goalie's place is in that abbreviated area between the posts. In fact, just about every man who has ever laced on the 40-pound leather pads has done his goaltending in close proximity to the cage. There is, however, an exception to this, and the following brief story tells of a goalie who ranged far afield with a rather spectacular result.

Chuck Rayner, who tended goal in New York — first for the old Americans and later for the Rangers — harbored an obsessive desire to spring away from his nets, dipsy-doodle through the enemy's defense, and score a goal against his opposite number on the other side of the rink.

During World War II, Rayner's fantasy was realized. Playing for an all-star Royal Canadian Army team, he was guarding the goal when a ten-man scramble developed behind his net. Suddenly the puck squirted free and slid temptingly in the direction of the other goal. What's more, there was nobody between Rayner and the puck.

The bush-browed goalie got the message. With a five-stride head start on his pursuers, Rayner charged down the ice. His opponents were so startled by the maneuver that they just stopped in their tracks to watch. What they saw was a phenomenon: Rayner skated to within firing distance and whacked the puck into the net. A goalie had scored a goal by skating end to end and then beating his opposite.

Left: "The Chicoutimi Cucumber" — Georges Vezina, the first great goaltender of professional hockey. He collapsed during a game, suffering from advanced tuberculosis, and died soon after.

Below: "The Shutout King," Terry Sawchuk, seen here stoning the Rangers. Sawchuk recorded 103 shutouts in his career, a record that still stands.

Roy "Shrimp" Worters, who measured 5' 3" and 130 pounds, was
the Hart Trophy winner in 1929 as the NHL's most valuable player
and winner of the Vezina Trophy (best goalie) in 1931.

Lorne "Gump" Worsley, whose long career was ended not by injury or age, but by a chronic fear of flying, made worse by NHL expansion.

Johnny Bower, seen here single-handedly holding the Rangers at bay, didn't land a full-time job in the NHL until he was 34 years old. After that point he took the Leafs to four Stanley Cup championships.

Billy Smith. "In the 30 years I've played and coached pro hockey," said Don Cherry, "there's never been a player who's wanted to win as bad as Smitty."

Ron Hextall. The fiery netminder returned to his first NHL club, the Philadelphia Flyers, for the 1994-95 season, after tenures in Quebec City and Long Island.

Tim Chevaldae recorded three hours of shutout hockey in the 1992 playoffs against Minnesota, when his team at the time, the Detroit Red Wings, were down three games to one and came back to win the series.

"The Dominator." Czech-born goalie Dominik Hasek beat out Grant Fuhr for the number-one netminding job — a feat in itself. Hasek went on to post some of the league's best numbers during the regular season for the Sabres.

Rookie sensation Martin Brodeur took his club, the New Jersey Devils, to within one game of the Stanley Cup finals in the 1993-94 season. His father, Denis, was the goalie for Canada's Olympic squad in 1972.

II

THE WAY IT IS

THE PLAYERS

-19-
Craig Billington

During the 1993-94 National Hockey League season, affable Craig Billington became known as the human dartboard as he faced shot after deadly shot in the Ottawa Senators net. To be kind, it was a dreadful year for the stopper who only a year earlier had performed nobly in the annual All-Star Game. Always warm and understanding, even Billington became angry at certain members of the Ottawa media who unfairly assailed him.

After all, the 1993-94 Senators rank among the worst teams in NHL annals with one of the most porous defenses known to man. With little to protect him, Billington nevertheless stopped about as many pucks as anyone could under the circumstances and finished the season with his head held high, though Ottawa held up the bottom of the league.

For Billington, it was a particularly disappointing state of affairs. Highly regarded after being drafted by the New Jersey Devils, Biller never quite could establish himself as a full-time big-league goaltender until the 1992-93 campaign. It was then, under coach Herb Brooks, that Billington actually annexed the number one netminding spot with the Devils in competition with teammate Chris Terreri. Named to the All-Star Team, Billington was playing the best goal of his life and seemed destined to remain a Devil for several years.

But goaltending is filled with surprises, and Craig became the victim of one such turnabout when the NHL expanded from 24 to 26 teams. Faced with losing a goalie in the expansion draft, Devils president Lou Lamoriello traded Billington and Troy Mallette to Ottawa for Mike Peluso and Peter Sidorkiewicz.

In one fell swoop Billington was transferred from a Stanley Cup contender to a second-year team with virtually no hope of making the playoffs. He accepted the move with professional equanimity, knowing at the very least that he would be numero uno in Ottawa, but also that he was likely to suffer the eternal goaltending disease known as "rubberitis" if he didn't receive protection from the Senators defense.

Ever the pro, Billington detailed his ascent from kids' hockey to the top during an interview with Ottawa reporter Richard Middleton. Craig's thoughts follow.

My goaltending life began when I was four years old and learned how to skate. We didn't have actual nets in those days, just a couple of rubber pylons that staked out the two goal posts. I kept gravitating toward them without knowing precisely what the lure of puckstopping was at that time, other than the fact that I just loved it.

Right from the beginning, I could tell that my psychology was different from the average kid's thinking who was playing hockey at the time. You see, most people duck when objects are thrown at them but the goaltender goes right toward the object, the puck. When the kids I played with would score a goal, they would jump up and down and make a big deal out of it while myself, in goal, would just get ready for another shot. So right there is the difference in psychology between a goalie and another position.

You can also see the difference just by looking in the *NHL Official Guide* or in a hockey encyclopedia. The forwards and defensemen are lumped together in one category and goalies are listed separately, as if we were a totally different species.

In any event, my parents viewed my young goaltending leanings with mixed feelings. My mother, who happens to be a kindergarten teacher, was more of a positive, psychological help to me although she never was too keen on hockey. In fact, over the years she's seen only about half-a-dozen games over my whole career. Nevertheless, she's always been there for support.

My father, who also is an educator and worked for the Board of Education for some 30 years, was the active parent in terms of taking me to the games. My father never put any pressure on me at all. He let me try everything, from hockey to baseball — whatever I wanted to do, and I can assure you that there were times that he had just cause to pull me out of the nets. As a kid goalie, I would get bombarded for 13 goals in a game — not that it's changed all that much — but it was a good test for me. Others might have become so frustrated under those circumstances, they might have given up but I decided that I would continue playing and, naturally, I'm glad that I did.

I'm sure that part of my thinking was influenced by heroes and favorite teams of that era. I always idolized Ken Dryden, who was then the star goalie of the Montreal Canadiens when they were winning all those Stanley Cups in the 1970s. I also was impressed by his intellect and the fact that he continued going to college and eventually became a lawyer. It was terrific how he managed with his education and also played hockey at such a high calibre for such a long time.

My career began in my hometown of London, Ontario, first on the minor hockey level, then on up to Bantam, Midget, Junior B and then away from home to Belleville, Ontario, which is a much smaller city than London. I didn't mind the change, especially since my mother originally was from a small city, so she prepared me as much as anyone can be prepared for such a change. Of course, you don't really find out what the switch is like until you actually experience it.

By the time I had reached Belleville, my priorities were pretty much in order. My immediate goal was to help the Belleville club win hockey games, but my long-range goal then was to eventually make it to the New Jersey Devils. If that didn't work out, I had decided that I would get an education. Long-range, I had my heart set on going into the business world. Even as a teenager, I thought about business, whether it meant dabbling in the stock market or running my own business.

I was very concerned about my education. When I was playing Junior hockey, I had concluded that a pro career could last only four or five years which meant that I could be out of it by the age of 25. Hey, your life isn't over at age 25, so you have to have something for a back-up.

My Belleville experience was a good one for the two years I spent there. I was lucky enough to win the Bobby Smith Award, which until then was the greatest individual honor I ever won. It shocked me more so than being picked to the All-Star Team for Belleville. Sometimes All-Star picks have as much to do with hockey politics as anything else but I was happy to be named to the team.

All in all, my Ontario Hockey League experience was a positive one, because the OHL is a league where you can combine education and hockey. To me it was the best league for pro prospects but it took a lot of stamina to hang in there. You're the on road three days and three nights. One night I was in Sault Ste. Marie and the next in Sudbury. There was a lot of travel, but it was all worthwhile because I finally got invited to come to New Jersey as a 19-year-old.

At the time the Devils didn't have that good a team, but they did have Chico Resch as their goalie and a nicer guy you'll never find. I spent time living there with his family and getting tutelage from him. It was a difficult time for the Devils organization because they just didn't have the talent, and it certainly was demanding on the goaltenders because of all the rubber we faced.

I knew at the time that I wasn't yet ready for the NHL, both mentally and physically. I worked on the strength part over the years, and the mental part also takes a long while. It takes time to fully learn the goaltending position and I was no exception. At 19, I wasn't finished growing and building my strength to compete at that level.

It's a fact of hockey life that it takes goalies longer to adjust to their job than it does for a forward or defenseman. Goaltending is a position that has to be studied and understood, which takes a while longer than for anyone else. Our position is more demanding than the others because we're the last line of defense and, consequently, we have to accept a lot of the responsibility. When a goalie makes a mistake, it usually shows up on the scoreboard.

A goalie, by the very nature of his position, also learns to be independent. By the time I was playing in Belleville, I felt that I was a loner. Not that I wouldn't do anything for my teammates — of course I would. But at the same time I liked my own space and when I got to the house that I was boarding at, I enjoyed my privacy. I didn't hang around with anybody in particular, just did my schoolwork and played hockey. I learned how to take care of myself, which meant learning how to cook, how to clean up the house and how to iron. No university class could teach me those skills.

It was a challenge in Junior just as it was in New Jersey and, most recently, in Ottawa. With the Devils, I was growing up with an expansion organization, and was with them as they became a successful and competitive club. It was very exciting and I felt that I was well respected there. Believe me, it was difficult leaving that kind of environment, going to another expansion team which was five to ten years away from being extremely competitive. I was starting from scratch, so to speak, all over again.

Obviously, a professional athlete can be happier in some cities than in others, and I was no different than anyone else. But I decided that I would make the most of my situation in Ottawa even though it wasn't going to be an easy experience. One thing I knew all along, and that was that I loved playing goal. If I wanted a genuine challenge, the job with the Senators was as good a one as I'd ever get. Every single night that I went into the net for Ottawa I had my hands full. But I survived the Devils expansion era, so maybe I figured that I could do the same with the Senators.

Someone mentioned to me that I'm older and wiser for my experience but I definintely know that I'm older; I can't say that I'm wiser. If anyone was going to give me some more smarts it was Chico Resch who, coincidentally, had become the goaltender consultant to the Senators and was in Ottawa when I arrived there. Chico knew me real well and was very supportive during the difficult times, always available to put a smile on my face.

Chico would remind me what I already had learned which is that it's a lot of fun to be a goalie, although on many nights it doesn't seem that way. I learned that you've got to love the game to get through the kind of frustration that many of us goalies do. Constantly we're striving for the perfect game — although it may never come — but that's something that's always on my mind.

What helped me along the way was the year I spent playing for the Canadian Olympic Team. The international experience taught me a couple of things, among them that there is a different style of play overseas with the wider ice. Playing over there, I came to respect the passing and the intricate European-style plays. I learned to read plays much better and have come to see how the NHL has integrated that formula into its system. These days you see a lot more "cycling" in the NHL than ever before. Instead of the old NHL up-and-down-the-wing method of playing, we now have more passing and more complicated plays, thanks to the European influence.

The other thing I learned overseas was the difference in customs among various nations. I discovered how other people lived other than Canadians and Americans. I learned how to adjust to different cultures. The sum total of the experience made me mentally stronger and tougher, particularly because I had to perform at a high level under Olympic pressure.

Looking back, I can say that the Olympic experience saved my career because it put things in perspective for me. It gave me a chance to work at my game and really appreciate the hockey business, where I was, and where I wanted to go from there.

It didn't hurt that I had some solid coaches along the way, including Dave King of the Canadian Olympic Team. Another who helped me a great deal was Tom McVie, who spent a number of years with me. I always say that anyone who survives a year with Tom McVie is doing alright. It seems as if I was with Tommy forever, but McVie taught me a lot and one of the most important things was to keep life in the proper perspective. The keys to success, he would say, include hard work, discipline and the determination to fight through adversity. He was notorious in the business for being a tough hombre, but Tom always was very fair.

One of McVie's virtues was that he made the game of hockey simple to understand. Another was that he could push you to a level that you may never have thought you could reach before.

In a sense, playing for Tommy helped steel me for what I would encounter in Ottawa but there are some circumstances that just can't be accounted for in advance. One of them is media relations. Throughout my career, I've had good interplay with the press. In fact, when I played for the Devils, I was given the Good Guy Award by the New Jersey hockey writers because of my cooperation.

But something happened after I got to Ottawa and I became known as a "tough ass" with the Senators. I base my relationship with people on the way I'm treated. I could be the best interview you ever had and I proved that with the Devils. I don't walk in and be a prick for no reason. There's usually a method to my madness. But I learned in Ottawa that you can't win with the media. The people who cover the Senators can be very difficult and, as a result, I can be very uncooperative at the same time.

Naturally, I put myself in a no-win situation because I don't write a sports column, therefore there's no way I can answer the criticism that I received with something of my own in print. Some might try to sweet-talk the critics but I'm never going to suck-ass to the people in the media who I don't like and who don't treat me fairly. At least those who deal with me know where they stand.

As for the Senators, we did the best we could, and I certainly tried my hardest. One of the problems was that we didn't have the size on defense to clear the front of the net. Dennis Vial was the best at that in 1993-94. But a lot of times it wasn't the defense. The forwards weren't holding up for them, allowing the D to stand up at the blue line. The system was just not executing, and that was part of my challenge. But one of the things I've learned is that I have to stay positive and remain a positive influence on my team. That's something I can control and something that has to be there, especially in the dressing room and around the guys.

I take a lot of pride in getting along with the people with whom I play. I try to help out my teammates whether I play one game or 60. I play from my heart with emotion, so one of the problems in Ottawa was that some of the people really didn't understand me. Certainly, the media didn't. But I also realized that I had to give them some time, which I was prepared to do. As long as both sides give each other a bit of time, things will work out fine.

Understanding is an important element in evaluating a professional athlete. Some fans believe that we pros take ourselves lightly, but I can assure you that nobody gets more upset with himself than the player. He's the one who comes to the rink, practices, works his tail off every day. He spends his summer working out in the gym and is the one who mentally prepares himself for each day. The player is the one who has to shave and look himself in the face. Nobody is tougher on himself than a hockey player.

Certainly, there are going to be disappointments. In Ottawa I was faced with many more quality chances against me but, on the other hand, it provided me with a greater challenge, which is what professional sports is all about. I believe in attacking the situation, make as many saves as I can and hope that it will all work out in the end.

I understand how the fans feel and if they boo, that's okay. People who pay from $30 to $100 for a hockey ticket can do whatever they want as far as I'm concerned, even though it may not be what we want to hear. After all, a fan has no other release than to shout.

Because of the nature of my position as goalie, it wouldn't surprise some people if I told them that I was superstitious, but I'm not. The game is tough enough without me going through all the rituals that a Patrick Roy does. I find it tough enough just to stop the puck without having to worry about other things. When they shoot it, I try to stop the puck and that is plenty.

Bear in mind that I am tickled with what I'm doing. The NHL is the best league in the hockey world and I consider it an honor to play here. Sometimes we lose sight of that fact and it's something I remind myself of all the time.

What I try to remember is that I'm among a select few of 600 players in the entire world and I cherish my position. I plan to make the most of it while I can, which is why I work my tail off every day to improve. I always say, be the best that you can be. If you're a fourth-line center, then be the best fourth-line center you can be. If you're going to be a goalie who plays only 20 games, fine, be the best 20-game goalie you can be.

I say, forget about everyone else's standards and focus on your own — what you want out of yourself. At least that's what keeps things in perspective for me.

-20-
Martin Brodeur

Martin Brodeur is the quintessential chip-off-the-old block. His father, Denis Brodeur, was a first-rate professional goaltender who starred on several minor league teams and also played for Canada's 1972 Olympic club which won a bronze medal.

Growing up in Montreal, Martin also had other advantages in addition to his father's tutelage. Upon his retirement as a player, Denis Brodeur became a professional sports photographer and worked Canadiens games at the Forum on a regular basis.

Thus, young Martin was exposed to the professional hockey life at an early point in his development and found that he was perfectly acclimatized to the ice scene. Employing his God-given ability and his father's guidance, Martin began a goaltending career in the amateur leagues of Montreal and eventually graduated to the top Junior league in Quebec province.

Brodeur played so well that he was selected by the New Jersey Devils in the 1990 entry draft with their first pick in the first round. Since the Devils were blessed with solid goaltending, it had been expected that Brodeur would remain in the minor leagues for several years.

But when the Devils opened training camp in September 1993, they discovered that their "second" goaltender, Peter Sidorkiewicz, was suffering from a serious shoulder injury and would be unable to start the season. Coach Jacques Lemaire decided to gamble on Brodeur as back-up for number one goalie Chris Terreri.

To everyone's amazement, Brodeur performed expertly when he was played, and soon found himself getting more and more opportunities. By mid-season it had become apparent to the media that Martin not only was a Rookie-of-the-Year candidate but also might dislodge Terreri as the Devils primary goaltender.

In a sense he did. Brodeur got most of the starting assignments during the Devils' run to the 1994 Stanley Cup semi-finals and played so well that he won the Calder Trophy as the NHL's top freshman.

Brodeur was interviewed at the club's South Mountain Arena practice headquarters in West Orange, New Jersey by reporter Susanna Mandel-Mantello. The youngster recalled his hockey growth and his maiden season in the NHL.

Even though my father was the Canadiens photographer, I didn't go to that many games at the Forum. I would listen to them on the radio or watch on television.

I actually started playing when I was three years old. At first they had me playing up front and I was very good. As a matter of fact, I probably would have remained a forward but one day our regular goalie didn't show up so I decided to try going between the pipes. Ever since then, I've been in the net.

Needless to say, I wouldn't have stayed there if I didn't play well but I took to the new position very well. When our coach asked me, "Do you want to be a goalie or do you want to be a forward?", I had no hesitation in answering. I said, "I want to be a goalie."

Ironically, my brother was a bit upset because he thought I would be a really good forward. I was so young at the time that I didn't even know about what a terrific goaltending career my father had had. Imagine, if I had told my coach, "I want to be a forward," I wouldn't be in he NHL right now.

This much is certain: whichever position I decided on was okay with my father, because the primary thing was that he wanted me to play hockey. The thing is, he wanted me to play just for the fun of it, not with any other motives. He never pushed me — just good, old fatherly encouragement. In fact, unlike other kids, I never went to a hockey school in my life. Maybe if I had, I would have got tired of hockey and not stuck with the sport the way I did.

Now that I had become a goalie, my father would observe me a bit more carefully. It was interesting because, despite his professional background, he never gave me a hard time if I played badly, but he would ask me questions about what I was doing. When he would ask me questions, I would come right back and ask questions of him — like, "How come you know so much about hockey?" That's when I began learning more and more about his background, and he told me everything and I suddenly understood what the bronze Olympic medal was all about. Up until then, I had never made the connection.

Once I had established that goaltending was for me, I went from one league to another — Bantam, Midget, on up — until I reached Juniors. I did well, although there was one incident that still sticks out in my mind. It was when I was playing in a Midget tournament and one that I really wanted to play well in, and there was this one situation when the opposition forward was coming down on me and the puck was out between us. I took a gamble and rushed out, trying to pokecheck the guy at the blueline, but I missed him completely. He just went around me and put the puck into the empty net. To this day, when friends want to bug me, they'll phone up and say, "Hey, do you remember that pokecheck you missed in Midget? " The funny thing is that that's one of the few things that I remember from my youth hockey days.

What I soon found that I liked about goaltending was the pressure; that you can always make the difference in a game. Even if a goalie doesn't have a great game, he can make the big save that will make the difference between winning and losing. I like making the difference in a game, and the goalie is the best person to do that.

From time to time every goalie lets in a bad one and when that happens, you just try not to think about it. When it's a tight game I have to really concentrate and look at the puck all the time. If I lose sight of it, that's when I get into trouble. If it's a tight game, I have to make sure that I only let in a "good" goal. A "bad" goal is damaging to your confidence. If it's a "good" goal, I say to myself, "Well, I did my best and that's it." Chooch, just like that, you erase it from your mind. You have to do that even if it's a bad goal, because the next one could be even more important.

Hockey is a mental game — that's the key. If you're strong mentally, everything will go right — I hope.

I had a big mental test early in my first season with New Jersey. It was December 8, 1993 when the Devils played Montreal at the Forum. Jacques Lemaire told me that I would be in goal that night which was quite an occasion and, as you would expect, the media made quite a big deal about it.

I must say that it was the first time that I ever experienced such an exciting feeling as I did that night. Usually, I'm not a nervous guy at all, but on this night I was pretty nervous. Once the anthems were over and the game started, the Canadiens took their first shot and my nervousness went away, just like that!

But it was something until that happened. You see, originally I was supposed to start for the Devils in Pittsburgh, but I got the flu so Chris Terreri started that game. That forced Jacques Lemaire to change the rotation and it meant that I would go up against the Stanley Cup champions in their own rink.

Once Jacques had decided to use me against the Canadiens, he let the media know that there would be strict rules. All interviews had to be done at the morning skate at the Forum and not before that. A couple of guys got around that and I ended up having to do some interviews just before the game, which I didn't like too much. I wanted very much to concentrate and all this was going to do was distract me.

Our goalie coach, Jacques Caron, was very helpful. Before I went out on the ice, he told me, "Don't try to do too much; let the puck come at you and take it easy." I was thinking that all the time, all day. I told myself, "Don't try to beat them; let them try to beat you."

It went pretty well for me; we beat the Canadiens and the next day I had 20 calls on my answering machine with people congratulating me. It was great.

Except for the fact that we were playing in Montreal, my pre-game preparation was the same. It's very important that I watch my favorite soap opera, *Days of Our Lives*. After that, I have to take my nap, but not more than two hours' sleep. If I sleep more than that, I'm too tired for the game. Then I eat a little snack, like a banana or chocolate bar, and I'm ready to go. The main thing is my soap and my sleep — that's it.

The problem is, when I play on weekends, *Days of Our Lives* is not on the air. What I try to do is find something else on the tube that catches my attention, but nothing can match my soap. What it comes down to is being in the best frame of mind for the game.

I do everything I can to help myself but there's always my goalie coach, Jacques Caron, available to help. He's always talking to me in practices and between periods during the games. He wants me to watch the puck, look at the puck everywhere on the ice and all the time. He wants me to stay on my feet as much as possible. I'm a big guy so if I stay on my skates, I cover a lot of the net. If I go down, I'm like a small goalie so it doesn't make sense for me to go down all the time. Sometimes it's okay, but not too much.

When I got to the NHL, I knew that I had the talent, but Caron's instruction has helped me improve on what I originally brought to New Jersey. My work ethic is very good. I love playing hockey. For me, being a professional goaltender is not a job; it's not like a nine-to-five thing. When I go to a practice, I could usually stay at least another hour after we have to leave — that's how much I like what I'm doing. Usually, I'm the last person to leave the rink.

My rookie season was funny. When I got to New Jersey and made the big club, I figured that I'd play a couple of games here and there and that would be it. The next thing I knew, Jacques was playing me every two games, which was really good. It gave Chris a rest and me too. That left us more sharp when we had to play.

What made it even easier was that Jacques' system emphasized defense and our defense played very well. When your club is good defensively, you don't need so many goals to win a game. When we would get a lead of two or three goals, we knew that we could keep the lead and win the game.

I like being a Devil. I go back to the day that they drafted me in Vancouver. Everyone said that I would be picked in the middle of the second round, maybe 30th overall, so it was a surprise and an honor to be picked in the first round. When my name was called out, I yelled, "Oh, yeah, wow!" It was hard to believe, and then moving up to New Jersey at the age of 21 and being so close to New York City.

Some players find that the big city is a distraction to them; I figure that if you want to make it a distraction you can, but I'm not the kind of guy who's going to go out and party. When I go to New York, I'm scared; I'm not sure of myself and where I'm going. The first thing I think about is hockey and after that I've got Atlantic City, New York, everything. It's great.

But I always have to keep in mind that my primary purpose is goaltending and I must do everything I can to perfect my job. I know that I don't have to be as strong as a forward, but I do need stamina and I try to be very well-conditioned. I bike and run, constantly work my legs. Hockey is a mental game, so I'm always thinking about that. Your mind is like your body; it has to work and work and work. Part of that work is communicating with teammates, especially the defensemen.

When one of my defensemen goes into the boards for the puck, I have to be sure that he doesn't get hit from behind. I talk to them as much as possible because I found that some goals just happen because of a lack of communication. A team with good communication is going to be a very strong defensive team.

My communication skills are getting better even though I was brought up speaking French. I learned English so well that when I would play summer hockey with my French friends, I would be talking to them in English and they would yell at me, "Hey, speak in French." But I got so used to speaking English that it came out perfectly natural for me.

As the 1993-94 season progressed, I developed more and more confidence. Part of it came from just looking around the league and seeing how former teammates of mine were doing. Felix Potvin was the starting goalie for Toronto, and he had been a teammate of mine in Midget hockey. Stephane Fiset had made the big club in Quebec and he, too, had been on our Midget team. Not bad, eh!

Which is not to say that goaltending was easy. There are too many good shooters in the league: guys like Mark Messier, Wayne Gretzky, Brett Hull. The way they score is unbelievable. Everything they do seems to create a goal or go in. It's unbelievable.

Even though I was a rookie last year, I got a lot of help from my teammates. Bruce Driver talked to me a lot and any time I got scored on, Claude Lemieux would come up to me and say, "Come on, kid, don't worry about it." The Devils took good care of their rookies.

I guess they started getting confidence in me when I won my first NHL game against Boston. I beat the Bruins, I think 4-2 and then 5-2 over Quebec. In my first game, I was picked the first star. That was some kind of blast for me.

Speaking of blasts, I'm often asked what it's like to face the hard slapshots that are thrown at us every game. Am I afraid? I'm more afraid in practices than in an actual game. In games a goalie doesn't have time to be afraid. I just try to stop the puck any way that I can. If I had to stop it with my mouth I would do it. It doesn't matter. I'm not afraid of the puck — not in a game. If you're afraid, you can't play the game. But when all is said and done, you don't have time to be afraid because the puck comes so fast. We're well protected and when it's going to hit you, it's going to hit you.

I also have learned a lot from my teammate, Chris Terreri. I learned just by watching him. He's steady and he knows every game he plays. He doesn't let in a lot of cheap goals.

Chris learned all about pressure a long time ago. I haven't felt much pressure myself. When I was a rookie in 1993-94 everyone was willing to forgive me if I didn't play all that well. But I tried my best to be as steady as a Patrick Roy. I figured that if I could do that, then my career would be great.

Another question that has come up to me is what it's like to be a French-Canadian in a mostly English-speaking league. There's no question but that it's harder for us as a group. When the average French-Canadian comes into the league he doesn't know the language as well, so it's all very different. I'll give you an example: if you take two players, an English-Canadian goon and a French-Canadian goon and there's one job available, they'll pick the English-Canadian because it's easier for him to talk to everyone and be friendly to all the guys. That's why most of the guys who come from Montreal and Quebec who are in the NHL are big stars. If they're not, the chances are that they won't make it as easily. They have to be really, really good.

People like me who come from Quebec like to stick together because the rest of Canada is always turning us down. I don't want to make a big deal out of it because whoever can do the job, can do the job. It doesn't matter if he's Russian, English or French. If a guy can do the job, he should be able to do it.

My dad was a good goalie but he never made it to the NHL because when he was in his prime, it was only a six-team league and most teams carried only one goalie in those days. When my dad played, goalies didn't even wear face masks. As a result, my father had about 114 stitches taken in his face. I can't imagine what it would be like playing without a mask in today's hockey.

Then again, it would have been hard for me to imagine back in September 1993 what the 1993-94 season would turn out to be for me, and all the great things that would happen, from playing at the Forum and winning to the playoff series with Buffalo, then beating Boston in the second round and, finally, the seven-game series with the Rangers.

I learned a lot from the experience. One lesson came from playing New York during the regular season. I didn't do well against the Rangers during the regular games but what I came to realize after the playoffs was that it doesn't really matter what happened in the past because you can only control what will happen in the future. Another lesson is that you can't let yourself get too down or too up; try to go with the flow all the time.

There were plenty of lessons from the playoffs, starting with the first round against Buffalo. Since I was a rookie, it was only natural for the Sabres to try to needle me and you can be sure that a lot of their guys talked to me, trying to get me off my concentration.

The highlight, of course, was the sixth playoff game with Buffalo at the Aud. That was the one that was 0-0 after regulation and then we played into a fourth sudden-death period. It's difficult to explain what it was like to be part of an experience like that. When I was playing, my concentration was so intense that all I was thinking about was finishing the game; getting it over with. Granted that Buffalo got the only goal, but I was still proud to be part of such a classic.

After the game, I was more mentally than physically tired. Actually, in the last two sudden-death periods, the skaters were so tired that neither team had that many shots on either goal so I had to work more with my mind than anything else.

When we went up against the Rangers, I felt very good about myself because the coaches, in starting me, gave me a lot of confidence. I went into the series really open-minded and played my heart out. In the seventh game, I gave up one goal in regulation and so did Mike Richter for the Rangers. I can't get down on myself for giving up the other goal in the second period of sudden-death. But it was really hard to take because when you play a close game like that, and you're so close to winning, you feel sorry and bad. What you don't want to say is, "Well, it's your fault or your fault." We were all in it together. All our guys played together throughout the series and we all lost together.

But there were so many happier moments in my rookie year. Winning the opening series against Buffalo was very important. When the coach picked me to start, a lot of people were saying, "Well, we'll see what the kid can do now." There were a lot of skeptics who thought a rookie couldn't hack it in a pressure situation like that. I showed them that I was capable of handling playoff pressure.

It all happened because early in the season the coach played me a lot and that gave me experience and confidence. Playing in Montreal and beating the Canadiens, playing me in the playoffs against Boston. Especially when Chris won the two games in Boston to tie the series at two, and then Jacques came right back with me in Game Five at home. Things like that are what I'll never forget.

On top of that, I came out on top for The Calder Trophy, which really made me feel good. I was thinking that the year before Teemu

Selanne won it after scoring 76 goals for Winnipeg, and then they voted for me the following season. Well, that was some honor because, to me, the Calder is the hardest trophy that you can win because you only have one chance at it in your entire career.

So now I have to build on that, but any time I see a problem coming toward me, I'm going to think about 1993-94 and what I accomplished that season.

-21-
Tim Chevaldae

Tim Cheveldae knows first-hand what a goaltender's roller coaster ride is all about.

When he became a Detroit Red Wing in 1988-89, the hockey world was his oyster. He soon became the darling of Joe Louis Arena fans and seemed destined for a long and lucrative career in The Motor City. A large contract signed prior to the 1992-93 season appeared to assure Cheveldae not only of security, but also longevity as a Red Wing.

But the Detroit fans — and media — are very demanding. Their club had not won a Stanley Cup since 1955 and the clamor for a championship sextet increased by the year. When the Red Wings were rapidly eliminated in the 1992 playoffs, Cheveldae was fingered for considerable blame and under the Scott Bowman regime in 1993-94, the pressure mounted on him to deliver big-time, or else!

Unfortunately for Cheveldae, the fans turned thumbs-down on him from almost the very beginning of the new season. If he missed a shot, Tim would hear the catcalls from the crowd more intensely than another goalie might under the same conditions. For Cheveldae, Joe Louis Arena became as hostile as any foreign rink.

The situation became so untenable that then-general manager Bryan Murray traded Tim to the Winnipeg Jets on March 8, 1994 in exchange for Bob Essensa.

Murray had staked his job on the trade. Essensa was supposed to do what Cheveldae could not do: deliver a Stanley Cup to Detroit. Instead, the result was disaster. Essensa failed miserably and Detroit exited in the first playoff round — to San Jose, of all teams — while Tim actually thrived in his new surroundings.

If nothing else, the episode demonstrated the instability of the goaltending profession. One can only imagine how much better Cheveldae would have played in the 1994 playoffs, had he remained a Red Wing and been available for the 1994 Stanley Cup round.

A personable performer, Cheveldae described his growth, happiness and hardship as a netminder to Detroit reporter Jim Ramsey. The following is Tim's story.

My hometown was Melville, Saskatchewan which is a typical small town on the Canadian prairie. The winters there are so long you really have nothing else to do other than play hockey, which is what I did.

To those of us who grew up there, Melville was a terrific hockey town and we treasured the fact that one of our own, Sid Abel, is in the Hockey Hall of Fame. Abel played for the great Detroit Red Wings teams in the late 1940s and early 1950s alongside Ted Lindsay and Gordie Howe. Sid was center on the immortal Production Line.

My father was a mechanic in town while mom stayed home and took care of the kids. I had two older brothers and one older sister.

In relation to the other kids in my area, I was a late starter. I began playing when I was seven and the way I wound up in goal was simple. I had hurt my leg and couldn't skate too well. In those days, they always put the kid who couldn't skate into the goal, and that was me.

Why did I like being a goaltender? Simple. In my first game I got a shutout. The coach liked me and ever since that day I was a goaltender. There were other elements that pleased me. The equipment, for one thing, was fascinating and, as a kid, I loved the attention that a goalie received. I have to admit that I liked getting a pat on the back before and after a game.

I was also into baseball and played on two provincial championship teams. On the side, I played badminton and volleyball.

My route to the NHL began in Melville, starting with the minor hockey program and eventually moving on to Saskatoon, where I played for three years. I always remember my stint in Saskatoon with a great deal of pride because even though the team didn't score a great deal of goals, we worked real hard. We were overachievers who lost in the playoffs twice to the eventual Memorial Cup champions, the Medicine Hat Tigers.

Then the Red Wings got me and I was sent to Adirondack (Glens Falls, New York) of the American League, where I spent a year and a half. That was my most enjoyable experience, because we had a great bunch of guys and won the AHL version of the Stanley Cup, which is called the Calder Cup. Glens Falls was a great place to play hockey because it was a small but lovely city, north of Albany, with a terrific rink and wonderful fans.

How tough was it getting to the NHL? Well, basically for a

young goalie, it's a matter of getting a chance. I was in the right place at the right time. I came into the Detroit organization at a time when the Red Wings goaltenders, Glen Hanlon and Greg Stefan, were up in years, hockey-wise, and the club was looking for a young goalie like me.

As it happened, Glennie and Stef both got hurt, which was bad for them but great for me because I got a chance to play with the big club. The biggest thing I kept telling myself was that as long as I got the opportunity to play a few NHL games, I could change my game and adjust to the league.

At every level you have to change your game and make adjustments to improve yourself and time is necessary to do that. Fortunately for me, the Red Wings gave me that time with a few call-ups. I got lucky. Once we went on a ten-game unbeaten streak with me in goal. The team was scoring a lot which was a blessing because they kept putting me back in. Another guy in the same situation might have kept on losing by a goal and would have wound up back in the minors after a couple of games.

Emotions play a big part in goaltending. At first I would get very emotionally high when I played well and get very low when I played badly. I couldn't control my emotions very well then. It's funny how you remember some things and forget others.

For example, I remember my first NHL game very well. We were in Calgary, playing the Flames. I had just got called up to the big club and Jacques Demers was the Detroit coach. He came up to me and said, "How's your game?" I said, "Oh, it's not too bad." Jacques came back and said, "Good, you're starting tonight."

Well, that was some news. Calgary had a really good club at the time and went on to win the Stanley Cup that year. When Jacques told me I was going to be in the nets, I said to myself, "Oh, God, here I am playing against a powerhouse and the game was going to be televised on *The Sports Network* and my family would be watching it back home in Melville."

That night I stepped on the ice and across the rink I was looking at guys like Al MacInnis, Gary Suter, Joe Nieuwendyk and Hakan Loob, all great players. I was in awe. I was thinking, "Man, what am I doing here?"

But it worked out well. I played a great game stopping 42 shots, although we lost 3-2 in overtime.

It was very interesting studying the faces on the other clubs, particularly in relation to the teams I remembered as a kid. When I was growing up, my favorite team wasn't the club that was now paying my salary; I rooted for the Philadelphia Flyers. I liked them because they were rough-and-tumble and were called The Broad Street Bullies. Dave Schultz was their tough guy and I liked his rough quality.

My favorite goalie in those days was Grant Fuhr who was playing for the Edmonton Oilers. He was so acrobatic and made so many saves with his quickness. From a goaltender's view, his style was particularly exciting.

Fuhr played for several Stanley Cup teams — something I have yet to achieve, although I have had some highlights. The best of all was in the 1992 playoffs against Minnesota when the Red Wings were down three games to one and we came back to win the series. I had over three hours of shutout hockey. Picking a low-light is really easy. It would be in the spring of 1993 when we went out in the first round to Toronto at a time when the fans had expected us to go so much farther.

Of course, a lot of exciting things happened in between and one episode I'll never forget was a fight I had with Curtis Joseph, the St. Louis Blues goalie, during a game in St. Louis in the 1992-93 season. The melee originally began with a one-on-one fight, which began escalating until it became a five-on-fiver. In the midst of it all, the linesmen took one of our players to the penalty box without taking one of their players. So it meant that now they had five skaters fighting and we had only four.

Anybody who knows hockey will tell you that there's an unwritten rule that says if your team is a man short during a fight, you can do anything you do to help even things out. Well, the one guy on our team who was outnumbered happened to be our best fighter, Bob Probert. I rushed to his aid, which is pretty ironic, you have to admit, and then Curtis saw me skating into the fray so he did his job and went after me.

Curtis caught me by surprise and jumped me but all he was doing was sticking up for his teammates. Both of us were just showing our teammates that we would cover their backs if they needed it.

The funny thing was that Joseph was embarrassed by what he had done to me, and I know this for a fact because we accidentally met a few days later in Tampa Bay. The Blues had been there for a game with the Lightning a few days before our game and then we came into town while they were still there. I happened to go to a bar that night and who should I see there but Curtis. As I walked past him, I said, "Curtis, can I buy you a beer? Can I get you anything?" He was sitting there with the other Blues goalie, Vincent Riendeau, and said, "I'm glad Tim is taking it so well." I knew he was really embarrassed about what he had done when he jumped me.

What I got from that fighting experience was a much greater respect for what guys like Bob Probert go through. My arms were so tired, you wouldn't believe it. And to think that a fellow like Probie had to do that every night. When you lose a fight, the fans are on your case. It's tough being an intimidator, although I must say that intimidation comes in a lot of different forms and not just from fighting.

Goalies are more intimidated by someone's hard shot. Like a Brett Hull coming down the left wing and teeing up the puck at the top of the circle can be intimidating. Same with other hard shooters like Stephane Richer, Al MacInnis or Mario Lemieux. Nothing is more intimidating to a guy like me than seeing any of them coming in on a breakaway.

Some of my critics have said that I'm too nice a guy to be a goalie — that I should have a mean streak and hack some of the players in my crease, but the fact of the matter is that that's not my style. Goalies like Ron Hextall have made careers out of being aggressive but I think an athlete should do what comes naturally. I'm like Kirk McLean of the Vancouver Canucks. We're not the aggressive types. Yet when you look at what Kirk did in the spring of 1994, taking the Canucks all the way to the seventh game of the Stanley Cup finals — and only losing by a goal — you have to admit that that non-aggressive style doesn't hurt. I find that if I worry about the defensemen or the player coming in, then I'm not concentrating on the puck.

Another aspect you have to take into account in evaluating the goalie's style is the way the game has been changing in the past decade. Hockey in the NHL keeps getting faster and quicker — more like European hockey. There's a lot more criss-crossing than ever before. When a shooter is moving in on the net, instead of looking to fire the puck, he's looking to pass to the back door for the tap-in. And with the increase in quick movement, the goalie has to be able to move in the net real well. I have to be more aware of the other four guys on the ice. There's tic-tac-toe hockey going on now that never went on before!

Naturally, shots have gotten harder and harder, what with the newer high-tech sticks. I can't imagine what goaltending was like when guys didn't have masks; I mean goalies like Johnny Bower, Terry Sawchuk and Glenn Hall. I guess they were always concentrating on not being hit in the face with the puck. Probably, the good thing then was that they didn't really know any better. I tell you what; if I had played in those days, and got hit in the face, it would really make me think about going out on the ice barefaced a second time.

Now we have the masks for protection but there's no mask that can protect a goalie from the wrath of a crowd. From my experience in Detroit, I can tell you that it can get pretty bad. Real bad. Lots of times the fans believe that you, the goalie, are the reason why their team lost. It figures because the goalie is in the position with the most power of any player on the team. On any given night, the goalie is the one who can single-handedly win or lose a game.

Not that I'm complaining, mind you, because this is something I grew up with and got used to over the years. A professional goaltender has got to learn to accept the criticism and learn how to deal with the fan abuse.

The most important thing is to be a good judge of yourself. I know when I play well and when I play poorly. A lot of times the writers in the press box will think a shot that gets by a goalie should have easily been saved, but we on the ice know differently. So, I have to be honest with myself and know how I played no matter what the others say.

The writers and the fans often believe that overtime creates a special kind of pressure for a goaltender and I wouldn't knock that. But by the time the overtime comes, I'm so immersed in the game that I really don't take it any differently. In overtime, the goalie already is sweaty and worked up and, to me, it's not a big deal.

That's the interesting aspect of goaltending; lots of experts have all kinds of theories on the profession but so much of it is instinct. Take the business of playing the angles, which is considered so important. No one can really teach you how to play angles, although a lot of work enters into the study of angles during practice. But once the game starts, the last thing you want to be doing when a shooter is coming at you is saying to yourself, "Am I square to the net?" No, I just want to react and not think. Sometimes I use the hash marks or dots to help me. If a shot goes by my skate a couple of inches and hits the post and goes in, it means I had my angle, but if it goes by my skate and ends up two feet inside the post, then I didn't have my angle.

Knowing when to come out of the nets and when to stay in depends a lot on the individual goalie. I like to challenge a fair amount in certain situations. Others, like Curtis Joseph and Felix Potvin, stay deeper in their net and feel comfortable with that. Lots of times it depends on the shooter. A guy who is not a big goal-scorer will come down the wing and bury his head for a slapshot and I can read off that, whereas a guy like Brett Hull will do the same thing, bury his head and try to make you believe he's going to shoot but then do something completely different.

If I'm playing a high-scoring club like the Penguins, I know that they're a good passing team and will be looking for a guy in a better position to shoot. As a result, I'll play a little deeper in the net for them. On the other hand, a club like the Blackhawks likes to shoot the puck and crash the net trying to create traffic and scrambles. I challenge more against them than I would against Pittsburgh.

When a club like the Blackhawks tries to screen me, I try to find the puck whichever way I can. I maintain that it's better to be out of position and see the puck than not to see it when you're in position. If I don't see the puck, I go down and cover as much of the net as I can, hoping that the shot hits me.

This comes by trial and error, same as the interplay between the goalie and his defensemen. The more I play with them, the more I learn where they want to have the puck set up behind the net. When Paul Coffey came to Detroit, I learned that he likes to pick it up on his backhand. When I stopped the puck behind the net for him, I left it three or four inches away from the boards. Brad McCrimmon liked for me to backhand the puck to him behind the net. Different defensemen like different things. Quite often, a goalie can't see which defensemen is coming and has to relate to the sound of his voice, but the more you play with them, the easier it becomes.

From time to time I've been asked what effect being pulled from a game has had on me. Actually, it depends on the reason I got pulled. Sometimes it happens when the team is playing poorly and the coach wants to light a fire under the whole club, not the goalie. Then, there's the mercy pulling. The team might be playing awful hockey and I'm getting shelled. In a situation like that, I'm happy to go. But if it's just me playing a bad game and I get pulled, I know that I'll have to do better the next time and I can't let it bother me.

Even with the masks and all the protection the modern goalie has these days, there's still an element of fear associated with the job of stopping pucks. For me, there's more of the fear element in practice than at other times, because in practice you see so many more shots than in a game and there's always the chance that the puck is coming up high.

When I get hit during a game, the puck may hurt, but the adrenaline is flowing that much more swiftly, so it blocks out the pain and enables you to make the sacrifice to stop the puck. Not so in practice. It doesn't mean a whole hell of a lot other than you're going to have ice bags on you afterwards. What I have to be aware of is the player who has the reputation for shooting high. When he comes down the wing, I have to keep saying to myself, "Stay down!" And I say it over and over and over again.

Scrimmaging with teammates is not the only way to keep sharp. I play baseball, tennis and other racquet sports, or I just throw a tennis ball against the wall. Soccer helps feet coordination, which is very important in goaltending. The biggest thing for any young goalie is to put emphasis on movement in the net, because the game has become faster than ever. The goalie has to keep up with the play, and that's why side-to-side movement is so important. Puck-handling is another skill that can't be emphasized enough.

Another facet of hockey that has changed dramatically is the use of the mask and the improvements made in its design. Masks can cost as little as $500 and as much as $1,500, depending on who is the maker. I've been using one designed by a fellow named Greg Harrison and it's as good as they come. It's a lot better than the old cage and helmet design that had two screws up at your forehead that connected the cage to the helmet. If you got hit with the puck it would drive those screws into your head, which is why a lot of goalies got cut even with the mask. The new masks are molded to the face, and the pucks are not likely to hit them flush but rather glance off the sides.

If you get hit on the cheek or chin with that kind of mask, it's still a little ways away from your face and pushes it in. The feeling is like getting slapped when your back is wet — you have a stinging feeling, but nothing major. I've been dinged a few times but never knocked out.

The other vital piece of equipment is the pads. My pair usually lasts about three-quarters of the season. After that, they get broken down and should be replaced. But I'm the kind of goaltender who doesn't like breaking in new equipment because it feels as if I have two-by-fours on my legs or a glove that I can't close. So, what I do is have my pads patched up when they break down and I wear them more than most goalies.

Unfortunately, there are parts of the body that simply can't be protected at all times. The inside of the thigh is one of them. If you get a shot there, it feels as if someone has drilled you in the back with a slap. We have padding on the arms but it isn't much and a puck travelling 90 miles per hour will cause plenty of bumps and bruises; and anything that hits around the groin area hurts a lot! Ditto for the collarbone. I know that they're making new equipment to cover it but it still seems as if there's always an opening the size of an inch that the puck seems to find.

Some of my teammates in Detroit will tell you that another piece of "equipment" that I had there was a mustard-colored sports coat. Here's how it came about: one day I told my wife to buy me a mustard-colored jacket, and she came back with a bright-colored yellow one for my birthday. I wore it once and then put it away in the closet and called it my "lucky jacket." It stayed in the closet until the Minnesota-Detroit playoff after we were down three games to one.

A few of my teammates suggested that I bring out the yellow jacket for good luck and I did. You know what happened? We won the next three games and the series.

But the jacket didn't do me much good in 1992-93 when the fans started to get down on me in Detroit. It reached a point where it was pretty hard to come to the rink. Life became frustrating for me. I didn't mind being criticized when I played poorly, which I did during the first half of that season. But I finished off with something like a 34-24 record which meant that in the last half of the season I went something like 20 and 7 and an average of about 2.50.

And I still was being criticized for not playing well. Well, people can see what they want to see and if there were going to see something negative out of the situation, that's what they're going to see, no matter what I was going to do.

That negative period had its effect on my family, although I must say that my wife was good about it. She had grown up in a hockey environment and she understood the entire situation. It was harder on my dad, my brothers and sister back home in Melville. They didn't understand that the media was going to write whatever it wanted and a lot of times my family took the criticism of me to heart. As a player, I understood that it was all part of the business of being a professional and that I was going to get good press sometimes — as I had earlier in my Red Wings career — and that I would get bad press as well. Sometimes it was deserving and other times it was not.

Naturally, it had an effect on me, personally. Sometimes I would take the game home with me, but I was fortunate to have a family. When I got home and saw my three-year old daughter, and I knew that she didn't care if I was the game's first star or whether I let in ten goals. I was just her dad and, believe me, that brought me back down to earth and reality.

As you can see, the mental part — be it at home or at the rink — is so much a part of the game. Perhaps *the* most important aspect during a game is the confidence factor. If you go out on the ice thinking that you're going to stop the puck, then 90 percent of the time, you will. But if you think you're going to let a goal in, you probably will. You have to go out there with a positive attitude and confidence level. A goalie has to have a little bit of arrogance about him. It's a position where everyone is going to see your mistakes and a lot of times you're either going to be in the doghouse or the penthouse. It's very much like being a defensive back in football. On the one hand, he makes a play and high-fives everyone and he's looked at as a cocky guy. It's like goaltending — you have to be cocky and arrogant to play the position.

When your confidence slips — as it does for everyone from time to time — the trick is to turn it around and the biggest thing, I've found, is to make the game real simple. I break down the first period into four segments of five minutes each and I say to myself, "I just want to get through the first five minutes without getting scored on," and if they score in the first two minutes, then I say, "well, they won't score for the next three minutes."

Goaltending is more mental than physical, but if you keep yourself in good physical shape, you're going to play well. If you keep yourself in good mental shape, you're going to play great. When I'm confident out there, I'm going to stop the puck most of the time. I just wish that I had that feeling every night but I try to program myself to get that feeling of confidence.

I also try to program myself to understand my opponents. When I play against the Blues, I am always aware of Brett Hull when he's on the ice. The same holds for Wayne Gretzky and Mario Lemieux. After a while, a goalie learns that certain players like to do certain things. When Hull comes in on a two-on-one the tendency is to think that he's going to shoot, but seven out of ten times, he'll pass across. A guy like Steve Thomas of the Islanders will usually shoot because he has such a great shot. When it comes to Gretzky, you simply can't cheat on him. If you overplay the pass, he'll shoot.

A lot has been made of videos as an aid, and sometimes I'll use it. If I play a good game I find it nice to watch myself and use the video as a confidence-booster. If I've played poorly, the video makes the game a lot simpler because when I'm on the ice, the tendency is to make it too complex. When you watch the tape, it seems so simple and it's nice to see, knowing that I don't have to change that much to get back in the groove.

With all the tension of goaltending, there are always some light moments that relieve the pressure. For me, one of the funniest things that ever happened surrounded the news that I was being called up to the NHL for the first time.

I had been playing in Glens Falls and got the phone call at about 1:30 p.m. The first thought that came to mind was, "Wow! My dream is coming true." Detroit had a game that night and my flight was supposed to leave at 2 p.m. It was a 45-minute drive from Glens Falls to the airport in Albany, New York. I still had to pack and pick up my ticket and equipment.

When I got to Albany airport, the plane was already on the runway. I had missed the flight. The next plane out wasn't leaving until 6 p.m. So, I got on that flight and it landed at Detroit's Metro Airport at 7:30 p.m., which just happened to be the same time that the game had started.

A policeman met me at the airport and said that he would rush me to Joe Louis Arena. Next thing you know, the police chief showed up and he said they would take me to the rink by helicopter. We went to a little airport and jumped into a police copter which flew directly to the roof of Cobo Arena, which is just down the street from Joe Louis Arena. The Red Wings trainer rushed out and met me, took me to the dressing room and I suited up between the first and second periods. Detroit had played the entire first period with only one goalie.

The second time the Red Wings promoted me from Adirondack another interesting thing happened. At the time, Greg Stefan was the number one goalie and he had hurt his back at the start of the year. Detroit was playing in Vancouver and I flew there from Albany airport. I got into Vancouver on Wednesday night for the game and when I got to the baggage area, none of my bags were to be found. I had hoped that the bags would show up the next day in time for the game. At the time that Stefan got hurt, our second goalie was Glen Hanlon, who had just about gotten fed up with his career. That day he announced that he was going to retire which meant that Detroit's number one goalie was out with a bad back and their second goalie was quitting. And I, their third goalie, didn't have any equipment.

Five minutes before game time our coach, Jacques Demers, went over to Hanlon and said that he had to play. Hanlon reluctantly agreed, while I was in the other corner putting on Stefan's equipment since mine hadn't shown up yet. Halfway through the warmup, my equipment arrived so I sat on the bench while Glennie played. He was wonderful, and after the game he told me that he had decided to go out there and just have fun. He did and he learned something from that experience; it extended his career another two years.

But neither of these incidents compared with the most embarrassing moment in my NHL life. That would have to be something that happened in Pittsburgh early in my career. I was pretty much caught up in the excitement of the evening, skated out on the ice and went directly to the crease where I busily started to "clean" it by skating back and forth, chopping up the ice. I did that for 30 to 45 seconds while the other guys skated around the rink. Finally, someone yelled to me that I was at the wrong end; I was in Tom Barrasso's spot. I had cleaned up Tom's crease in front of 16,000 people.

-22-
Darrin Madeley

The sky could be the limit for Darrin Madeley who, at the start of the 1994-95 National Hockey League season, found himself in position to soon be the number one Ottawa Senators goaltender.

But there remains a big IF involved.

Madeley made a strong, positive, impression filling in as Craig Billington's back-up during 1993-94.

In a season virtually dominated by negatives in Ottawa, Madeley emerged — along with Alexei Yashin — as one of the few positive elements in the Senators' future plans.

Whether he has the goods for long-term success remains a moot point. Certainly, he will be given every opportunity by the Senators to become their goalie-of-the-future.

In the meantime, he finds himself in a position similar to 1994 Calder Trophy-winner Martin Brodeur — except that Madeley has lacked the personnel in front of him to make winning easier.

We chose Madeley for the book because he represents a goaltender on the brink of success but one who still must lift himself over the last major league hurdle.

Ottawa reporter Richard Middleton interviewed the affable puckstopper who readily explained how he got into the business and how he enjoys it.

My hockey education began outside of Toronto along with Curtis Joseph of the Blues. He was a year older than me and played on the same Peewee team. I was five when I actually played goal for the first time. It was simply a case of nobody else on our team wanting to go in the nets, so I decided to give it a try. I did it well enough to continue in the nets, although I liked playing other positions as well. The thing was that I found more success playing goal than the other positions, so I decided to stick with what was working for me.

By the time I reached my teens, I was still playing, but not all that well, so I decided to concentrate on school and go to Ryerson [University] in Toronto. It was then that one of those strange events took place that can change a person's life.

Before heading for school, I played in a junior tournament at Richmond Hill in Toronto. I played pretty well in my first game but got beat 6-0 in the second one against the St. Michael's club, which was powerful at the time. I figured, okay, I got my couple of games in and I'll go to school now and forget it.

But the night before school was supposed to start, some scouts came over and started talking to me. When I told them I was going to school the next day, one of them told me to think about it overnight and talk to my parents, which I did. They pointed out that I might regret turning down the hockey opportunity and convinced me to give it a try.

I took their advice, and even though I played for a horrible team, I got plenty of experience and pretty soon some American universities began talking to me. One of them was RPI in Troy, New York and the other was Lake Superior State. It turned out that RPI was using me to get another guy, so I chose Lake State, which gave me a 70 percent scholarship.

What a move that was for me. I was All-American twice and Player-of-the-Year. In my final semester, we topped it off with the National title. Now here's the irony. Remember, I mentioned that RPI wanted another goalie ahead of me. Well, I found out that that guy didn't even play in his senior year — he sat on the bench.

My goaltending improved significantly at college. Before that I was an average goalie who would sit back in the net and wait for the shots to come. In college, I learned to be more aggressive and think more about the game, diagnosing plays and whatnot. The other advantage of my college education was that I met my future wife there.

Yet, even though I was a two-time All-American, none of the NHL teams seemed interested in me at first, but then we won the national championship and three clubs — the Bruins, Kings and Senators — got in touch.

The clincher for Ottawa was after [GM] Mel Bridgman flew my wife and myself to town and gave us a tour. We found that it had the atmosphere we were looking for, since L.A. was so big and so is Boston. I'm from a small town and the big cities kind of threw me off a little. Besides, I was looking for a team that would be patient and was willing to send me to the minors to learn the trade.

Ottawa sent me to their American League farm club in New Haven in 1992-93 and that was the perfect learning situation for me because we gave up a lot of shots. That gave me a lot of experience and a hint of what I could expect on an NHL level. Or, at least I thought I would get an idea of what the big league was like.

But when the Senators promoted me to Ottawa I found the jump unbelievable. In the NHL, everyone can shoot hard and they do great things with the puck. I found it frightening at times to know that people can shoot the puck so hard.

Still, I was lucky in one sense, and that was Ottawa having Chico Resch as their goaltending coach. Now, I had known about Chico going back to his goalie days with the Islanders and later the Devils and I always liked the style he played. I'm more of a stand-up goalie and Resch encouraged me.

When I came to training camp in September 1993, the Senators had Craig Billington and Daniel Berthiaume as their one-two goaltending combination. But I came into camp with the attitude that it was Berthiaume's job I was after and I had to take it away from him. I was consciously thinking that I had to out-goal this guy every time we're on the ice together.

I honestly felt that I could beat him out and I felt that I had a good training camp. I was very motivated, and eventually I did make it. But even after I got to Ottawa, I didn't harbor any illusions. I knew that I still had to learn the league and that I had to be consistent.

First of all, I established a plan. I made it clear to myself that I wasn't going to go out there and dive around like I was the greatest thing in the world. I naturally wanted to keep the games low-scoring and play so consistently that people wouldn't notice me out there half the time; that would tell me that I was playing a solid game. I don't like getting on my knees and throwing my arms up in the air, knocking and waving. I prefer being stand-up solid, making the saves look easy. Since I'm not the biggest guy in the world, that's how I've got to play.

In that regard, the two NHL goalies I love watching are Felix Potvin and Bob Essensa. Potvin is just so smooth and makes everything look so easy. That's why I can't wait to play Toronto, being on the ice at the same level, watching Felix.

So far, in my brief big-league career, my number one thrill was beating the Canadiens at the Forum in overtime. It's funny because, as a kid I rooted for Montreal and also for the Maple Leafs, which is about as stupid as you can get. When the teams played each other, I had to ask myself, "Now what am I going to do?"

Of course, that was long before Ottawa got back into the NHL, but now that the Senators are in business, I've developed an appreciation for the city and its fans. They're very knowledgeable and know if you're working hard or not.

In some cities the fans can be very tough on a goalie, and I'm glad that Ottawa fans aren't like that and, hopefully, never will be. When the fans start getting on a goaltender, he loses a lot of confidence. I know I feel like, "Oh, God, don't let them shoot at me anymore or those fans will get on me."

It's ludicrous for fans to behave that way. If they want to help their team, they should try to do it in a positive way. But I'm not naive enough to think that everything goes the way we'd like it to go. I know from personal experience because I had to put up with charges that I was frail. Naturally, I had a few injuries in college but they got blown out of proportion, unfortunately, and I phoned up Senators GM Randy Sexton and had a talk with him about it.

When I got to the NHL, I once got a slapshot off the shoulder but I stayed in the game. Another time, I was sliding across the crease to make a save and I popped my shoulder. At the end of the year I got caught with a guy skating behind me. I stuck my leg up to make the save and got the post just when he took me the other way. So, I was getting caught with a bad reputation from injuries that were unavoidable.

Because I'm small, I'm going to get run over a lot. Why, I even read about ankle injuries that I never had. I'm just trying to get the record straight. One year I got drilled in the balls with a shot. It was flukey but there was nothing I could do about that. Getting hit there had nothing to do with the way I'm built. Everybody's got them and they're going to get hit.

Or the time I got clipped with a cheap shot; I was out to play the puck and the guy slashes me in the back and kicks my feet out from under me and I go flying. Now tell me if there's a goalie alive who wasn't going to get hurt, considering the air time I had. I was pretty high in the air before I came down.

Or the time the puck hit me in the head. I mean, if I get out of the way of it, the puck goes into the net and the other team has a goal. Or the one with my wrist. It means that if I get out of the way, the puck goes off of my shoulder. Or the fellow who takes my leg with him after I make the save and the net wouldn't move. If the net had popped off its hinges the way it was supposed to, I might have been all right.

No, I'm not going to change my style. I'm going to get hurt from time to time but I'm not going to change the way I play the game. I'm not even going to worry about it as long as the coaches know I'm working hard and the injuries are legitimate. I have never faked an injury in my life and I'm never going to fake one.

My opinion is that all this injury stuff got around because the newspapermen are looking for something to write about. Like when I first came up to Ottawa there was stuff in the paper about how I was supposed to be frail. Well, I got to the major league level at this weight and I can't get any bigger than this. There's nothing I can do about it. I can't blame my dad, who was a big football player, so let them blame my mom, who is built like me.

Look at Eric Lindros — he's way over 200 pounds and way over six feet tall but he's had two knee injuries in two years because that's the style he's playing. He's going to hit you as hard as he can every night and just because he gets hurt doesn't mean that he's frail. It just means that he's playing hard. If you're not playing hard, you're not going to get hurt. Same with Wendel Clark. He's had a bad back but look at how he goes at everybody, every night.

It's fascinating for me to be goaltending against players that I had once watched and admired on television when I was younger: Wayne Gretzky, Mark Messier, Steve Thomas. When I get on the ice against Adam Oates, Cam Neely and Ray Bourque, it's still unbelievable to me, but I also have to make sure I'm not afraid of them. Like in my rookie season I was scared to death of Pavel Bure when we played against Vancouver. Every time he got the puck, I was saying to myself, "Oh, God, somebody hit him."

That proves that I have to mentally make sure that I go at these guys and not away from them. If I back off of these guys, they'll score on me. When I play in the Forum, I don't see who I'm playing against. I don't want to be thinking about Guy Lafleur, Larry Robinson and those guys. If you start thinking about ghosts and not the players on the ice, you're in trouble.

In college, I used to keep a "book" on the shooters and then I decided to stop doing it and I wound up having the best year of my career. Now, I don't even think about who we're playing against and I'm pretty relaxed before a game. I don't start thinking about the game until the warmup. Once I'm out on the ice, I start thinking. If I did it before, I'd have an ulcer by now.

Let me picture something for you: let's say Mario Lemieux is coming in on me with a breakaway. I'm thinking, "Okay, what's he gonna do?" He doesn't know what he's going to do, so how the hell am I going to know what he's gonna do? And with the talent he's got, he's gonna score 900 times. I've got to make sure that I get lucky on one of those ten.

I remember a night in Winnipeg when Teemu Selanne came down in the final seconds of the game all alone on me. I found out later that he was one of the best breakaway players in the league. It was like, if I had known that, I would have been crying in the corner somewhere instead of making the save.

The interesting thing about that game was that I knew only one guy on the ice, and that was Nelson Emerson and that was because I had played against him in college and I knew how fast he was. It's good, in a way, for me to be aware of him as long as I'm not afraid of him.

What it all comes down to is that I have a great respect for anybody in this league. The way I figure it is if you made it to this league, you're a pretty darn good hockey player. To be an NHL goalie, you've got to be among the top 52 in the world. That's overwhelming enough. Then I think about the fact that I'm in the world's élite league, and that heightens my respect even more. I don't care if they're physical players or great scorers, they've got *something* to be here. About 30 years from now, I will be able to say to my kids that I played in the NHL, and that's a statement that not many people in the world would be able to make.

Not bad for a kid from Holland Landing, Ontario where the population goes over 500 only when a lot of people come to town.

-23-
Rick Tabaracci

For a time there was good reason to believe that Rick Tabaracci would become the lead goaltender in Winnipeg, but it wasn't to be. The Jets traded him to Washington in 1993 and Tabaracci instantly won critical acclaim at US Air Arena with a series of impressive performances during the homestretch and in the 1993 playoffs against the Islanders.

Tabaracci was on track to become the Capitals go-to goalie in 1993-94 but, again, injuries broke his progress. Instead, Don Beaupre split puckstopping duties with occasional appearances by young aspirants such as Olaf Kolzig.

Nevertheless, Tabaracci is still young enough to establish himself among the NHL elite although, admittedly, he must demonstrate more durability than he has in the past.

Washington reporter Mary McCarthy interviewed Tabaracci following a Capitals scrimmage at their practice rink in Piney Orchard, Maryland. Tabaracci's thoughts on his goaltending life follow in question-and-answer form.

Q: Did you start life as a goalie?

RT: No. I switched when I was about 11 or 12. I was a center until then. I'd never played goalie before. Except I have a brother who is four years older than me. If I wanted to play hockey with him and his friends, I ended up being the goalie but only in road hockey games.

Q: So you had experience!

RT: Yeah! I put it on my resume when I applied. I always wanted to play goalie. But my parents wanted me to skate. They always wanted me to play "out," which really helped me to develop hockey skills.

Q: Then you knew how to skate really well by the time you went in the net?

RT: I did. And a lot of that even helps me now. I'm able to see plays happening and see the ice a little better. I was playing with the Toronto Young Nats, a Triple A team, and playing center, and one day in practice I just went in net. It ended up going pretty well, so we switched.

Q: You went right to that level? Started playing goal at the Triple A level?

RT: We started halfway through the season and they said, "Well, chances are you'll play a few games but you won't play many and you certainly won't play in the playoffs. But by the time we went to our first tournament, I had played all the way through the tournament and played all the playoffs that year, as well.

Q: Were you afraid of the puck at all when you first started goaltending?

RT: Unfortunately, no, although I wish I had been. *(Laughs)* Maybe I wouldn't have been here now. No, seriously, it was a different position and I always liked it. There was a lot of pressure to goaltending, but it was also a lot of fun.

Q: It sounds like your family was really involved in your hockey from the start.

RT: They're still my biggest supporters and fans. Especially my brother and my dad. When I was young, my mom would take my brother and me to our games. And toward the end I'd look up and my dad would be there. He'd come right from work. No dinner.

Q: You grew up in Toronto, so there was a lot of hockey right there. No need to travel around much.

RT: Yeah, but the travel was the most fun. We'd go on trips to four or five tournaments a year. We had some really good people involved in our organization. Allen Sherman was our manager for a long time. He's still coaching. We had a good relationship with the people in Detroit, Compuware. We'd do little weekend things where we'd go up and be billeted with their families and then they'd come and we'd do the same for them.

Q: How did you learn the job of playing goal?

RT: I was fortunate having a lot of people around who could help. When I first started, Gavin McRae was another guy who worked with our team. He was a trainer. When I started in net, my dad told him to find me a set of goalie equipment as cheap as he could because they were still thinking I was gonna change back. So he went out and got full gear, head to toe, for $150 bucks! Used equipment from some guy in Toronto. So I put that stuff on. Gavin McRae always helped. And another guy, Stu Guthrie, he helped. Stu's a good friend. We've kept in contact. His kids are starting to play now. But we've always been so lucky in Toronto because there have been so many people really involved who go the extra length to help.

Q: Did you go to summer camp to learn goalie skills?

RT: A little bit. Mostly when I was a forward. Yeah! Ha. That was another time! I went to Seneca College in Toronto for a hockey camp. All week we'd work on the skills and they'd invite the parents in to watch the game. Well, I was there as a centerman. And I skipped an age group, so I was playing with the older ones. My parents were real proud. And they came to watch the game, and they couldn't find me anywhere. Finally, I took my helmet off for a second and my dad said, "He's in the net!" Oh, they were mad. They said they'd paid all that money to send me there to learn how to skate and the other stuff and there I was in net.

Q: What made the big difference in your development? How did you get head and shoulders above your age group?

RT: A lot has to do with the fact that you're given certain abilities. Like Kevin Hatcher and Al Iafrate. They're gifted. They've got abilities to do things that other players, no matter how hard they work, won't be able to do. In a sense, some of those are important in goaltending. Maybe you're a little quicker getting across, or you're up and down. Things that certain players have. Playing up front helped me a lot, too as far as reading the players and understanding what's going on the ice. One of the biggest aids was, since I was 13 or 14, I lifted weights, and I've done a lot of sports, especially track and field. And I always worked hard at what I was doing. That's probably the biggest thing.

Q: Your hobbies are listed as water skiing and motorcycles. You're not another one of those Harley guys, are you?

RT: No. I had a Yamaha Virago. I've taken a couple of trips, one from Toronto to Winnipeg. I love motorcycling. Now I've got an old car. I got rid of the bike. I'll probably pick up another one sometime, but I've got a 1966 Mustang convertible. I had a guy fix it in L.A.

Q: Did you have coaches in the Ontario Hockey League who helped you particularly?

RT: Orval Tessier was my coach in Cornwall. The biggest thing he did for me was giving me a lot of games. I had a ton of games. Sixty out of 66 in one year. Always a lot of games.

Q: So that's the best way? Get experience?

RT: Yeah. We never had a great team there. So I was getting 30 or 40 shots every game. Sometimes I got a lot more than that. But you almost have to take a step back when you get into pro hockey, because now you're not getting a ton of shots. You've got to learn to stay focused, and keep in the play without a lot of work. So, when I got to the NHL, it was almost going backwards a little bit.

Q: Is that difficult? The concentration part?

RT: That's the hardest part of the game for us. If you're in a game where you're getting 40 shots, you're going to be in it all the way. If you're in one where you're getting 20 shots and they get 14 or 15 good scoring chances, that's a tough night. Because you're out of it for 10 minutes, and then you get 3 or 4, and they're gone again for another 10. The mental aspect is the toughest part for a goaltender.

Q: Do you ever glaze out and start thinking about your car or something?

RT: Yeah. Sometimes you're watching the play. All of a sudden you're analyzing the play. You think, "What if we did this? Or, we should have done that. Back to work!" Yeah, it happens. You've got to be real careful that your mind doesn't wander.

Q: Goalies have unique pressures among hockey players because you're more visible. Do you find that difficult?

RT: It's harder after the fact. For a while in 1993-94, we weren't scoring many goals. So first you're competing to get in the net. Then, once you get in the net, you're competing not to let anything in because you want your team to get the upper hand first and then see what happens. Finally, the game is over. We once lost a game 2-1 to New York just before Christmas — and it was a tough feeling. I was thinking, "Well, what if I'd stopped the puck on that one shot? It would have made a big difference." Or, "What could I have done?" So it's tough. There are only two of you, and there's a lot of competition to get into the net to start with, and then to stay there.

Q: Almost every goalie has real down periods — you're the goat, then all of a sudden you're the hero. And it can change almost overnight.

RT: The beginning of 1993-94 was like that. We lost six in a row. I came back, all of a sudden, we win four out of five. We lose the next four. You can look at your record and you're even four and four. And you think, "Now what?" And all of a sudden things start to change again. Because you're not winning, it doesn't matter how well you're playing. Especially in a situation like this where you've got two goaltenders . . . and Donnie Beaupre is a capable goaltender. They're not going to say, "We're not going to play him." You know, they're going to change it up. They're going to feel comfortable. So it's a situation where you either win or you don't play. Coach Jim Schoenfeld is the kind of guy who's going to do that. Whoever's hot is going to play. Which is great. That works better for every goalie. There isn't one of us who is going to say he wouldn't like to do it that way.

Q: When you came here — first you got traded, which is kind of traumatic — then you came here and got two shutouts your first six games. Isn't it hard not to get pretty excited about such success?

RT: Yeah, it is. As much as anybody, I was caught up in it too. All of a sudden I go from the last year in Winnipeg when I was the guy who was playing all the time. When it came to the playoffs, I played all seven games. The next year, I'm back to one out of four games. And for no apparent reason. It just happened. They felt more comfortable with Bobby [Essensa]. You come here and then you're thinking, "Well what if the same thing happens again?" But they laid it open pretty wide and said whoever is playing well is going to play.

Q: Did you and Donnie Beaupre talk about it?

RT: Yeah. Donnie and I sometimes talk about it. We even laugh about it. We were in a situation before the All-Star Game where we both got shutouts, and didn't play the next game. And that was something Terry Murray did for the first time during that season. Cut and dry, you're going to rotate for two weeks. So for whatever reason, that's what he did. But you're saying to yourself, "What's going on here? This doesn't seem right." That's when we were sort of laughing about it.

Q: Do you worry more about the ones that shouldn't have gotten in, or the tough ones that you think maybe you might have stopped if you had done something different?

RT: You worry about the questionable ones. There's a certain line. I once let a shot in from outside the blue line in Boston. I mean, it was a decent shot, I looked over and I thought I had it, and it started to go a little bit, and all of a sudden it's going over wide and it's in the corner. And you're thinking, "Oh man!" It's one of those goals you think you should have had. You get up and you're thinking about it and you say, "What can you do, it's in." But it's the ones where you're a foot farther back in the net than you think you should have been, or you didn't react or follow the play the way you could have; those are the tougher ones. You know, I can look at a tape and see things I do when I'm really playing well and focused. And if I don't see those things on the tape, I know that's what I have to work on.

Q: Are there particular shooters who are trouble for you?

RT: The obvious ones. Mario Lemieux; Brett Hull's got a great shot. Guys with quick hands. A guy I've always had trouble with is Petr Klima, for some reason.

Q: Because he's sneaky?

RT: He's real patient with the puck. And he's pretty accurate. That's mostly when he was out in Edmonton. I played against him a few times out there.

Q: Who has the hardest shot, other than Al Iafrate?

RT: He's definitely got the hardest. When he was in Washington and we'd scrimmage he was pretty good, though. He kept it low. He was one of the better guys in practice. Al MacInnis has a hard shot. A French kid out in San Jose. I've seen him score from outside the blueline a few times. Russ Courtnall has a good shot.

Q: What are you working on now with your game?

RT: It's more a matter of staying in line with what I do and make sure I don't change from game to game; just keep the consistency going from one game to the next. As far as what you're doing, technique, style, how much you play the puck; with my style of playing, you have to have really good communication with the defense. We all go out behind the net and lay the puck out where a guy normally would pick it up, and because we're not communicating now, one of their guys picks it up. Then all of a sudden you see the play's real scrambly. And it doesn't have to be that way.

Q: Do you talk to the defensemen when you see that going on? Do you say, "Hey guys!"?

RT: The best thing I can do is be their eyes. I try to yell at them all the time, tell them when a guy is coming on them, which way the puck is going.

Q: What can a goaltending coach do for you at this point?

RT: It's good to have one for feedback—and we had a great one in Winnipeg in Dave Pryor. I really enjoyed working with Dave. He wasn't just a guy who was going to analyze for you, he was always on your side as a goalie. Not just mine. He was on Bobby's side too and Mike O'Neill's. He would always go to the wall for you because he felt strongly about your abilities. And he gave you a lot of confidence, and that's the biggest thing a goalie coach can do, because we are in a different position and we take a lot of heat.

-24-
Don Beaupre

Talk about venerable, do-the-job goaltenders and Don Beaupre automatically comes to mind.

He burst into the NHL at the start of the 1980s and virtually carried Minnesota's North Stars to the 1981 Stanley Cup finals against the New York Islanders.

Beaupre has, for the most part, been an efficient big leaguer ever since. Because of his almost fragile physique, Beaupre was considered a short-term prospect in the bigs. Yet he survived well into the 1990s, most recently with the Washington Capitals.

Washington reporter Mary McCarthy cornered Beaupre for a free exchange on goaltending and his career. They chatted at the Caps' Piney Orchard practice facility in Odenton, Maryland. The question-and-answer session follows.

Q: Were you always a goalie?

DB: When I was seven years old, I played three games at center and then I went to the net, and I've been there ever since. I only let in one goal my first game in the net, so it seems that's where I was meant to be. It was when I was seven that I started playing organized hockey. Everyone just signs up and says, "I wanna be a center. I wanna be a right wing." No one really knows what they should play. They tried a few kids in goal, and I did well so I just stayed.

Q: So you liked it?

DB: Well, when you're successful right away you like it. We had a pretty good team, won a lot of games and I stopped a few pucks.

Q: I remember you saying that you come from a hockey family. Did anyone else play goal?

DB: No one else, but it was a hockey family. My brothers played. My dad coached. It was a family activity. My sisters played ringette.

Q: You weren't scared in goal?

DB: No. I can't remember being scared at all.

Q: Well, that must be a prerequisite for playing goal, that you not be scared.

DB: Well, at times *now* I am. Sure. In certain situations. If a guy shoots high, and you're not in a position to defend yourself, it's kind of scary.

Q: Because pucks really hurt, don't they?

DB: There's no doubt. Every day you get a couple that hurt.

Q: People think pucks don't hurt because of all of your equipment.

DB: Well, you should know that you're not going to get hurt real bad. It's going to hurt, but you're not going to get hurt bad. You know that and trust your equipment from playing a few years. But it still is scary sometimes.

Q: How did you get goaltending coaching when you were little?

DB: When I was in Peewees I went to hockey schools three years in a row. Two were in my home town [Waterloo, Ontario] and one not too far away. And the same goalie coach was at all three. So over the three times, I learned a lot of the fundamentals from him.

Q: Was this a college coach?

DB: No, he was playing in the Senior League at the time and he was very respected. His name was Boat Hurley. He was a real quiet guy, tall and lanky. I don't know where he got the name "Boat." There's been a couple of other guys who are playing in the league who grew up in the same area and he coached them, too. He taught me the fundamentals. You know, angles, the different basic moves. Just working with him over that period of time helped a lot.

Q: Obviously your family was investing a lot in your hockey by that time.

DB: My parents gave me lots of encouragement. My dad was always supportive, but most of all he was just real proud of what I did, and that gave me encouragement to do more. He was involved in the hockey association that ran the school where I went twice when I was in PeeWee, and that's about the only reason I got to go to that school. The third time I went to hockey school, a neighbor wanted me to go with him because his parents wanted help with the driving, I guess. And it turned out that the same coach was there.

Q: What age group did your dad coach?

DB: Squirts. Ten and eleven. So when I started at seven to eight, I thought I'd really like to play forward. But at that point my dad was managing the squirts and he said if I stayed in goal, I'd have a really good chance to make this Squirt team the first year. So I thought, well, I probably won't make it, I'll never get to play on that team. I had grown up watching them, going to all the games my dad coached, and I thought those guys were like NHL players, because they had pretty good teams all the time. So if playing goal was the only way I had a chance to make it, I decided I would stay in goal. I made the team and I got MVP of the team both years. Obviously, I wasn't going to change after that.

[N.B. *It is absolutely clear by looking at Donnie's eyes dance as he recounts this part of his life that he looks back on his career as a Squirt with tremendous pride. In fact, I would say that he is more proud of that accomplishment than being in the Stanley Cup finals, All-Star teams, etc.*]

Q: Did you take power skating lessons?

DB: No. My friend's dad built an outdoor rink and he built boards and screens, and put headlights in his backyard. We built a real nice net and took good care of it. We skated all the time, and on Wednesdays I went to public skating. I took my skates to school and went right to the rink.

Q: Did you ever play with other guys who ended up in the league?

DB: Wayne Gretzky played in my league. A lot of guys came from his town.

Q: Then during high school you went to Sudbury?

DB: I was going into grade 12 and I moved to Juniors. Then I was going to split up grade 13, take six credits each year over two years just to give me something to do. But then I didn't play the second year of Junior. So I didn't finish grade 13. But I got my high school diploma. I guess it doesn't matter too much now.

Q: How about your development after you got into the OHL?

DB: I played Junior B first when I was 15. I was playing with 21-year-olds. That was a big jump from minor hockey to Junior B because the players are much bigger. But that made it easier to get to Junior A. There's still a lot of mistakes made in Junior A in the OHL. Everyone kind of fits in and grows together and develops.

Q: How about coaching?

DB: Our coach was a goalie, so he understood. He was a real players' coach. If there was a dispute between a player and management, he took the player's side. Which is right in Junior. You've got a lot of young kids away from home for the first time and they've got no one on their side. So if you've got the management, and the media and everyone against you, it's tough. So it was really good for us as players. We really worked hard for him and were successful.

Q: Did the coach give you more goaltending instruction?

DB: A little bit. But mostly he just let me play. We didn't have a real defensive team then, so I saw a lot of action.

Q: When did you begin to believe that you could make it to the NHL?

DB: Not until my after my first year of Junior. I knew it was tough. I had to establish myself among that peer group of goalies in the OHL to see where I fit in. I felt then that I was as good or better than most in that group.

Q: Do you think a lot of goaltending "talent" is really just natural instinct?

DB: I think so. It's just wanting to stop the puck. Some guys have the drive to stop the puck, and to do whatever it takes to stop the puck. But there's really a fine line between being a *good* goaltender and being a *great* goaltender. You want to make all the saves. And if you do, you'll be a great goaltender. You know, a bad goaltender lets in pucks he should stop. And a good goaltender stops all the ones he should stop. And a great goaltender stops the ones he has no business stopping. That's the difference.

Q: Yes, but a lot of shots are physically impossible to stop.

DB: Exactly! You have to separate those from the others. But if you're really sharp, you do have some kind of a chance on all of them. You can turn that chance into a save. Sometimes the guy shoots, you stick out your arm at the same time and the puck hits your arm. A lot of it is luck, but the fact that you took the extra effort to stretch out your arm, that's the difference!

Q: Are you still learning about goaltending?

DB: I work on what I know. That's part of maturing as a goaltender. You have to learn what things work and what things don't. In your first few years, you don't know what you can get away with. Now I don't catch nearly as much as I used to. And I get my body out a lot more, and play the angles a lot better than I used to, and stand up a lot better.

Q: You're very even-tempered. A lot of goaltenders I've talked to talk about the struggle to deal with the ups and downs of the job. Tretiak said if he had it to do over again, he never would have become a goaltender. For every goalie I can think of, there have been ups and downs. Isn't that true?

DB: Yes. For me, to be up and down, if I don't show it on the outside, I am feeling it inside. It's a job where you always have to react to what someone else is doing, and it's not just the other team. Your own team, too, dictates a lot of what your job is going to entail that night.

Q: But goaltenders have it tough. You can go from washed-up dog meat, so to speak, to hero of the week in no time at all.

DB: It's all balance. Unless you're in your 40s, you don't deteriorate physically that much. And if you do, you compensate by playing smarter. I used to think you had to be all wired up and jumping all around the net to play well, and I've learned that's not always the best way. You have to be more even in your temperament. You're not going to last too long if you're wired up like that. Take Ron Hextall as an example: I can't believe the energy he expended just in warmups. Jumping around when there's no play, let alone what he does in play. I really didn't think he could last doing that and I think he slowed down on that stuff a lot.

Q: You mean you think he's burned out?

DB: No, I just don't think you can keep that up night after night, year in and year out, and expend that much energy. The season's too long and it's too tough mentally and it gets too tough physically when you're playing 60 games per year. Maybe you can do it, but your level of play really drops off.

Q: Is being such a nice guy a plus or minus on the ice? Put the question a different way, you are a nice guy, but not always on the ice. I've seen you go after your teammates and tell them when they're goofing up.

DB: I don't go after them. In practice when someone whizzes one by your ear, then you go after them. Playing goal is the toughest job out there. But defensemen, when they've got plays on all sides of them, that's awful tough. Goaltenders play 60 minutes. The defense, they may be scrambling. But then they get a whistle; they're tired, they go off. Five more guys come on. But the goaltender stays and faces it all again. Then, you get a situation when a goalie gives up a bad goal. You could make 50 saves but even if you lose 1-0 and you give up a bad goal, you're the goat. But once you realize you're a goalie, that's what you have to accept.

Q: Ken Dryden talks in one of his books about staying awake after a game, thinking about the pucks he let in. Does that ever happen to you?

DB: If it's really an important, intense, emotional game, I'll wake up in the middle of the night, thinking about a goal that went in that I could have had. But as you get older, you learn to put those things behind you.

Q: Who are the best defensemen you've played with?

DB: Rod Langway was the best defensive defenseman. When I first got to Washington from Minnesota I couldn't believe it. I never played with anyone like that who just seemed so big in front of me. And that really impressed me.

Q: How about the shooters. Hardest shot?

DB: Every team has a couple of guys who can shoot it. Sometimes the guy you think has the worst shot can let one rip and blow it by you. I remember one goal against St. Louis in 1992-93. We were up 4 to 1, or 5 to 1, and Brett Hull took a pass at the top of the circle. And I barely moved. I just kind of moved a bit to the long side, kind of off the post. I hardly moved. And it was over my shoulder, up in the corner on the short side before I knew it. It was an overwhelming shot. Just a great shot. Hard to believe he could get it away that quick and into that little area. He does it all the time, so how do you argue with results? It was an overwhelming shot, from a spot where you didn't think you could make a shot like that. I've had guys come down the wings and blow 'em by me, slapshots. But that's different. So I'd have to say Brett Hull has the hardest shot. He just let it go.

It was just an overpowering shot where I had no chance to react.

Q: Who's the most deceptive shooter?

DB: Pat Lafontaine. You think he's tied up in front of the net, but all of a sudden the puck comes at you. And he's good at kicking the puck from his skate to his stick and getting the shot away.

Q: Gretzky or Lemieux — is it intimidating to see either one coming toward you?

DB: There's no doubt, they're both tough to stop. But I really enjoy playing against them because it's a huge challenge, especially if you're playing well. It's not so much fun if you're not real sharp.

Q: Who did you really hate to see on the ice?

DB: I remember the Islanders at their best. Mike Bossy, Bryan Trottier, Clark Gillies, Denis Potvin. The power play was awesome. Pittsburgh's is now, too. But I remember those Islanders my first year. Then again, probably the most overwhelming every time you played them was Edmonton when they had all their top players, after they had matured. It was scary.

Q: Was it scary playing in the playoffs in your first year in the league?

DB: No, not at all. I'd always played in playoffs growing up. It all kind of progresses. The year started when I made the North Stars and I wasn't supposed to make the team. So I got a lot of attention for a while. Then I made the All-Star team. And I got a lot of attention from that. Things went real well, and I was feeling real confident in my game. Then we made the playoffs. We won a round. Then we won two rounds. Progressed like that. Then in the final, you realize the whole hockey world is watching you and you remember when you weren't in the league and you were watching. And it is a real good feeling.

Q: Why aren't fans more appreciative in Washington?

DB: The Capitals went through some tough times after some high expectations. The Caps didn't perform up to expectations in the playoffs. To get the interest and to grow, you build up expectations, but don't leave fans disappointed.

Q: Every year you come to training camp, you're like the top gunslinger with always someone out looking to replace you. So you make it through the process, then you end up one of two goaltenders. And you're always in a sense competitors, aren't you? Then you became the senior guy. Do you help your partner?

DB: Yeah you do, by being friends. I always think, "You can't play all the games anyway. It takes two of you." So one is going to play more than the other guy. And you're both out there trying to play the best you can, and to be the top guy. But the decision is up to the coach. The coach can make or break a guy. He can play you a lot and if you have a decent team, you're going to be the top guy. And if you have a bad team, you can play a lot and look like the worst. A lot has to do with the coach. So if you don't play, you don't really have a beef with the guys who's in the net. You meet with the coach if there's something you don't agree with. A lot of times it's because you're not playing well. But I would never get mad at another goalie because he's playing. He's just doing what you want to be doing. Then again, if you're playing all the games, it doesn't help to be negative toward him either.

Q: How does a goalie decide it's time to retire? When Mike Liut left, I thought he had a couple more years left in him. Did he talk that decision over with you at all?

DB: No. His back was really hurting, that was it. I have no idea how you decide it's time to retire. Maybe when your back hurts. Or your head hurts. But as you get older, they're always looking for the young guys to get in there playing. So there's more than just play that can change your status with the team. You always want to be the top guy because the top guy has security. It's easier to move the second guy.

Q: Do you think money has become a detriment? The longer you play the more you cost?

DB: Oh, yes. Sometimes a club needs to trim the payroll but they have to do it smartly. If you're trying to trim construction costs, you don't begin by getting rid of all your best tools.

Q: Is there any difference in the way GMs conduct their business? Are they maybe less people-oriented because of the money aspect?

DB: Yeah, it's changed. Management has changed and the players have changed. The players used to take what management says as gospel. Now everyone wants to find out for themselves. This is because a lot of guys have played in college and they're more mature when they come in and they question things. Also, tradition has been thrown out the window a lot in the last few years. Before, you'd get paid in succession of seniority. That's changed. So management is less interested in keeping people around who are making a million or a million-and-a-half just for old times' sake. You can't run a business like that. But I think that's for the better. If you play ten years in a sport, you should be able to retire. But that wasn't true of hockey. Now the money may shorten careers. We'll see. Maybe the drive isn't there. We'll see.

Q: What do you think about the influx of East Europeans?

DB: The talent level has gone up. But they don't come over to win the Stanley Cup, let's face it. And no one can expect them to. They come over here to earn a lot of money and that's the motive. Again, management saying winning the Stanley Cup is what they're after isn't always realistic. After you have financial security, then that kicks in. You can do both. You can want financial security and the Stanley Cup. But the East Europeans, they don't have the Cup in mind.

-25-
Kay Whitmore

Kay Whitmore is the back-up goalie's back-up goalie. After an enthusiastic build-up with the Hartford Whalers, Whitmore was relegated to secondary status and remained on that level until being dealt to Vancouver in 1992.

As a member of the Canucks, Whitmore performed his second-banana role under first-stringer Kirk McLean as well as coach Pat Quinn could have hoped.

It was Kay's misfortune — if that term can be used — to play behind one of the NHL's best puckstoppers. He did that as well as anyone could in 1993-94, but looked on as Vancouver took New York to the seventh game of the Stanley Cup finals.

Nevertheless, the Canucks appreciated what they have, secure in the knowledge that Whitmore is a winner. Kay was the epitome of graciousness during an interview with Vancouver reporter Sandra MacPherson. The question-and-answer format reveals much about goaltending and the goalie.

Q: Recall the first time you stepped on the ice.

KW: We lived out in the country, in Sudbury, Ontario and my grandparents lived right on the lake. Every year we'd clear the big rink and all the kids from school would come over and we'd have the pucks out and play until dark. Just like the typical Canadian boy. It actually did happen. Some years there would be no snow, so the whole lake would be like 12 miles of a big hockey rink. You could just skate forever and ever. That's where it started when I was really little. My first season of organized hockey was in a playground, outdoors. I got my equipment on in the back of the car. Stood out there and froze. Probably lost 17, 18, 19-1 because our team was the worst. This was when I was six or seven.

Q: But you still really liked it.

KW: I liked it or I didn't know any better. I must have liked it.

Q: How old were you when you first stepped on the ice?

KW: Soon after I started walking. Your parents teach you how to swim and to skate right away. Seemed like it was just a given thing to do.

Q: What about brothers or sisters?

KW: I have one brother, four years younger, Keith. We were always at odds, battling all the time. He'd always have a friend over that was his age and I'd always have someone over my age. It would never be one of the younger guys and one of the older guys. It would be the two guys ganging up against the two young guys to try to win. Street hockey or ice hockey or driveway hockey. It would get really rough, actually.

Q: Beating up on your poor younger brother?

KW: I had to then, because he's bigger than me now.

Q: I recall a story in the Vancouver program that said you remember playing hockey in the basement with Keith. He would be in net and you would be shooting at him. When did the transition take place? When did you end up in the nets?

KW: I was always the goalie in organized hockey, but when I was a kid, we'd play downstairs when a game was on TV. We'd only come upstairs for the intermissions to watch "Peter Puck" or "Showdown" and all that. We had the ultimate basement. It wasn't finished, it was all cement with a big wall and big nets. Keith didn't mind going into the nets and I liked to shoot. It was fun. We'd play when we couldn't do anything else. We'd play two on two. Our basement was big enough. We'd set up boards and we'd have two nets. Tennis balls all over the place. I was a big Boston fan. I had a jersey and I got my mom to sew a number four on the back. I had a little mask that I put the stitches on like Gerry Cheevers had. My brother was always an Islander fan. And he used to drive me nuts. He liked them before they won all those Cups. And it would just bug me because they'd always beat Boston in the playoffs and he'd just gloat about it. He loved Bryan Trottier and Mike Bossy. I'd think, "God, why does he like these guys?" And then they were winning and it would really bug me.

Q: What about goaltending equipment?

KW: The first year I played outdoors my parents rented it or borrowed equipment from the little community shack. I was fortunate. My parents did very well and we were able to have good equipment. We never brought brand-new stuff; we usually were able to get some second-hand stuff when I was young. I grew so fast that I kept just growing into a bigger size all the time. I'd just follow some guy in town. He'd just keep passing his stuff down. That's the way it went until I was about 16. That was a big thrill to get my own set of custom-made goalie pads for myself. Everyone had them and they had to be "Brown's". It was like, "You're going to be a goalie if you get a pair of these things."

Q: Did the Whitmore brothers have any infamous stories to tell like the Sutters or Plagers?

KW: There was enough of an age gap. I left home when I was 16, and at that time I guess he was 12. I haven't spent that much time with him in the last ten years. He's been away and I went away to Junior and then I turned pro and he went away to Junior. Our paths crossed a couple of times during the summer. It's kind of sad. We really didn't spend that much time together.

Q: You were pretty active in basketball during high school.

KW: I was just a little guard who used to move the ball up the court and pass it. I didn't learn any moves until about grade eleven when I used to play pick up. I couldn't hit a basket if I tried when I was in grade nine.

Q: At what point did you feel you might have a chance to turn pro in hockey?

KW: My dad was quite a hockey player in his day. He was a big high school hockey, football guy. He went on a scholarship to Middlebury, Vermont. I heard he could have turned pro, but I think it had something to do with myself. My parents have never told me the whole story. From all the clippings I gather that he was supposed to be pretty good, and I just wanted to be like him. I guess he kind of regretted the fact that he didn't get a chance to go pro, so he pushed me a lot along the way. There were times when I really resented it, but then I don't know if I would be here if he didn't push. If I had a bad game, he'd let me have it on the way home. After a bad game, my parents would come separately from work. I would always want to ride home with my mom. If it was a good game, sure I'd ride home with dad. He meant it in a good way. He just wanted to see me make it and he's very proud now.

Q: You played your Junior in Peterborough.

KW: When I was there, we had a very, very tough team and just had unbelievable success. Oshawa, where Kirk [McLean] played, was about 45 minutes up the road. It's a General Motors factory-working town, and half of Peterborough commutes there every day. At work you're got half the guys wearing the Oshawa Generals shirts. They're betting all day about the game. At the game it's just a zoo. There's a lot of bad blood and brawls. I was 16 and I get out there and all of a sudden everyone is fighting. It was like what is this? It was a pretty scary situation, but I got used to it. The fans were great and both teams were always really good. I wasn't scared to go in there, but I knew I was in a hell of a game.

Q: You remember Kirk McLean being the opposing goaltender.

KW: Yeah, 'cause I played all the time and he played all the time. So every night we were battling against each other. Now we're pretty good friends.

Q: Who were your coaches in Peterborough?

KW: Dick Todd was the coach the whole time I was there. He was great, just a stop-the-puck kind of coach. One year I was there, Jacques Martin was an assistant coach and he worked with the goalies a bit. That was my first year and the next three we didn't have a goalie consultant. Dick was great. We had such good teams in Junior and everything went so well for myself that he didn't really have a problem that I had to worry about. He had a great open-door policy where you could come in to spend more time in his office after practice. Dick listened to what the guys used to say. He really appreciated your input. That's why we were so successful.

Q: This may be a stupid question, but what makes an NHL goalie?

KW: When you're young, you get a lot of the fundamentals — stand on your feet, keep your stick on the ice, challenge the shooter. You get that drilled into your head for so many years when you're Atom or PeeWee. When you turn Midget, when hockey starts getting a little more serious, when you start getting scouted for Juniors; at that point you're playing on God-given ability and I was so lucky that I had that because that took me right through Junior. I was a reaction-type goaltender. I used my reflexes. I had quick hands and that, until I started turning pro. Then I got to work with some guys and I started to watch different styles, began to learn the game. A lot of it's happened in Vancouver, with Glen Harlon and Kirk. We had goalie coaches in Hartford, but what they were saying just didn't work with my style. Every thing has just been perfect. I'm learning the game more and more. When you learn your angles and stuff like that, you can combine it with your reflexes and it makes you pretty good.

Q: Has there been anyone else who has been a great deal of help in your career?

KW: There was a hockey school that I went to every year, from when I was little to when I was 16. It was put on by Dave Tatarin, who played for the Toronto Toros for a while. He was with the Rangers. He bounced around a little bit. He knows more about goaltending than anyone I've ever met.

Q: In 1985 you were drafted by Hartford in the second round, so I guess you knew you had a good chance of going high.

KW: There was a lot of hoopla because there was Sean Burke and Troy Gamble and myself. Mike Richter was in that draft. There was a lot of talk that goalies could go in the first round. You knew you were going. They said come to Toronto where I had a lot of meetings with general managers the night before. They wanted to see what kind of guy I was. Rogie Vachon said, "We're not sure. We have two picks in the first round. We're not sure we're going to pick a goalie. We're not even sure if a goalie is going to go in the first round. But, if someone takes a goalie, whenever it is, then they're all going to go." As it turned out, they waited until the second round and then bang, bang, four in a row. So, he was right on.

Q: Were you glad to be going to Hartford?

KW: I was just so happy to be going anywhere, it didn't matter. I actually had no preconception of where I wanted to go. When they said Hartford, I just said, "Great!" It's a team. Anywhere, it doesn't matter. I was happy to go there. I was sitting in the crowd. The first-rounders are all standing up and shaking hands with everyone. It was kind of nerve-racking for a while. Then I went down and put the sweater on. I met everyone.

Q: Tell me about the feeling when they finally announced, "The

Hartford Whalers are proud to select from the Peterborough Petes goaltender Kay Whitmore."

KW: I stood up and then wanted to run down there. I was meeting all these people and shaking all the hands and now I can't remember anyone. You're in such a fog. You're so excited. You've got the sweater on and you've got the hat on. You're just so proud. You're shaking everyone's hand and then they sit you down at the table. My mom and dad were there. It was special. Unfortunately, they had separated a couple of months before the draft, but they made do. They came together and it was a great day. We had a big dinner after so it was exciting that day.

Q: Who were the goalies in Hartford at the time you first came to camp?

KW: Mike Liut was their number one guy. Steve Weeks was his back-up. Peter Sidorkiewicz had played a lot of games for them in Binghamton for a couple of years. They had some other draft picks who had been asked to training camp as well. Steve Weeks was my first roommate that year at camp. He was just the greatest guy, treated me so nice, made sure I had someone to go to dinner with. You're 18 years old and going to your first camp, all you are is tired. The guys are just so fast. All you want to do is sleep. He really took care of me, and we're still good friends. Mike was good to me too.

Q: They had a goaltending coach there?

KW: The last two years I was there, they had Jacques Caron. He's working for New Jersey now. He played way back, in St. Louis. He was a big help to me when I was in Springfield, the year we won the Calder Cup. He turned everything around for me. He was a big part of that.

Q: That team in Springfield — were they a favored team to win the Calder Cup?

KW: When I went down there in November, we were .500. I didn't expect to be there very long. They said go down there and play some games. Thirty-three games later, I went back to Hartford for a couple at the end of the season and then back to the AHL playoffs in Springfield. That was one of the best teams, as a team, the I have played on. It jelled at the right time. We had guys like Mikael Andersson, Marc Bergevin, Terry Yake, James

Black, Yvon Corriveau. Springfield was a funny team. When I played in Binghamton it was such a drag. Everyone wanted to go up so bad because we weren't very good. But when I played in Springfield we were such a good team we almost won every night. You didn't even think about going up. You just played and won. And then we went on that run through the playoffs with the greatest bunch of guys, a bunch of practical jokers. You'd be sitting in the bathroom stall every day and someone would pour baby powder over your head. Marc Bergevin, he would do that every day. I never had so much fun, and I still feel so close to them, but I haven't seem them pretty well since the parade the day after we won it all.

Q: So you had a parade?

KW: It was a pretty big deal, but not so much a parade as a big gathering. The mayor was there and a lot of people were there. It was unbelievable, definitely one of the best moments in hockey that I've ever had; the first championship I'd ever won.

Q: What about the final game of the championship?

KW: We were up by two and we were just cruising along and Bill Houlder dumped the puck in and it took a real funny bounce. He shot it from just inside center and it went through my legs. The whole crowd just hushed. We were to wrap it up that day. It was at home and everyone wanted to see it. Everything was going so well for me and all of a sudden the crowd just went quiet. Then, right away they started clapping. I could hear hundreds of people yelling, "Don't worry about it Kay, just hang in there!" It was just so great. Then we got an empty-net goal and the biggest celebration after. It was just wild. We sat there for a couple of days and couldn't believe it. June 1st and we were still playing hockey.

Q: When you played your first NHL game, did you have any idea you were going to be called up?

KW: No. Our coach was Claude Larose. I had played almost 60 games that year in Binghamton. They were going on a mini-trip and my leg was a little sore, so he said to just stay home and rest. Relax for a couple of days. I thought that was great. I'd just hang out. Then five minutes later he comes running in and says in his French accent, "Come in here, come in my office! You're going up, you're going up!" I said, "Going up

where?" "You're going to Hartford for the rest of the year!"
"Really?!" "And you're probably going to play Wednesday!" I
just went, "Wow!" So I packed up as quickly as I could, and
Larry Pleau was the Hartford coach and he said I was going to
play the next day against Boston. How ironic. That was back
when Hartford used to have the big crowds. The fans were all
out there. Playing against Boston, that was a huge rivalry, too.
It turned out they hadn't beaten them all year. And we won 4-
2. The Bruins had Craig Janney, Ray Bourque and Keith
Crowder. Keith actually scored one of the goals.

Q: Does a goalie always remember the first NHL goal scored
     against him?

KW: It's as plain as if it happened yesterday. It was the second
     period. Five minutes in. Janney was behind the net and he
     threw it out front. It hit the back of my skate and went in, off
     my own skate! Then, the same thing in the third period. They
     dumped it into the corner, it came flying out and he came
     skating right into a slapshot and it went in right off the post, 3-
     2. And then Kevin Dineen put it into the net and we won 4-2. I
     was the happiest guy. I wanted to kiss him, I was so happy. I
     wanted to win that game so bad. My teammates were really
     trying as hard as they could for me to win. Sometimes players
     may resent young guys coming up. I didn't really know the
     guys that well. I'd only met them through training camp. You
     don't really get to know them. The older guys hang together
     and the younger guys hang together. They made a seat for me
     in the dressing room between Dave Babych and John
     Anderson. These are two of the nicest guys that you'll ever
     meet in hockey. They kept me loose right up until game time.
     We were laughing and joking and talking. They'd say, "Hey
     you're not a normal goalie, you're talking and everything.
     You're not hiding in the corner." "Yeah," I'd say, "I think I'm
     normal." They made me feel really good. Then the guys played
     just incredible that night.

Q: Of course your first playoff game was against the Canadiens in
     the Forum.

KW: It was my first time ever in the Forum. First time I have ever
     walked in it. And the team regarded my debut there as such a
     big secret. They didn't want anyone to know who was going to

play in net. I knew way before, but they didn't want to release it to the press. Larry Pleau told me that I was going to be starting in Game One. It was the day before that I found out, but we went through the whole charade. We said, "Peter's probably playing. We don't know who's playing." He even skated out first in warmup. I have the game on tape and broadcaster Dick Irvin is all of a sudden going crazy because there is some new kid in net. He's going, "Shades of Ken Dryden." And all that stuff. It didn't turn out that way, but it was pretty thrilling that first night. I was making brilliant saves that I don't even know how I made in the Forum, in the playoffs. A kid that had played three games in his whole career starting the playoffs.

Q: What's it like playing in Montreal's Forum?

KW: When you go to the Forum you just feel the history, you absorb everything, the fans, the whole city. You just can't wait until 7:30 when that game starts. Sometimes at Hartford it wasn't that exciting to start the game, but once you got started you were fine. You weren't just standing there at the anthem, like in Chicago, where you're just champing at the bit to get going.

Q: How would you keep yourself from getting up too high before a game like that? For me, I'd just be a nervous wreck. I'd be shaking.

KW: It's funny, you're like that until you get on the ice. The worst part is the waiting. And once the game starts, instinct takes over and you play. But during the anthems and the introductions, especially in Montreal, there is so much press and hoopla.

Q: Who were some of the Montreal players?

KW: Russ Courtnall was there, Brian Skrudland, Bob Gainey. The nucleus of the guys who won the Cup. They were a good team that year. They beat us four straight. I played in Game One and Game Four when we lost in overtime. That was one of the best games I've ever seen, back and forth. We were all over them but Patrick Roy stoned us; the shots were something like 46-41 but we just couldn't buy a goal. We had so many chances to win that game. And then I ended up throwing the puck up along the boards and Russ Courtnall batted it out of the air. He ended up sliding it into the empty net with a whole bunch of us diving. That's how our season ended with a whole bunch of us lying on the ice. Four-game sweep.

Q: Can you put into words your feelings at the time?

KW: I just couldn't believe he had the puck with a wide open net. No one was going to get it. I just dove and it seemed like time stopped. Everything went in slow motion. I just dove and then I just lay there. That was probably the worst moment. I felt like I had let the guys down that I really didn't even know yet. Because I was so young, I felt like I had blown everything. That was probably one of the saddest moments. Tears came to your eyes pretty quick. But the guys were great. They came over and patted me on the head and said, "Hey, you played a heck of a game. It could have been over a long time ago if you didn't make all the saves you did." The reporters were great, too. They thought this kid is going to go hide in a corner and never come out because he's just so mad or embarrassed but I just came out and talked to them. That gained a lot of their respect because I talked for as long as they wanted.

Q: How frustrating was playing in the minors?

KW: I felt I had done everything. I had played 60 games, I had won all kinds of games. But I kept going back there, until I finally took the team to the championship and got my name on the Calder Cup. Then they finally realized that I was ready. I played almost 200 games in the American League. There were times when I was miserable and I wanted to get out of hockey because I didn't think I would ever get out of there. But, that year when we won the Cup, it did it for me. It did it for Wendel Young. He went with Hershey and won it and he hasn't looked back since. Once you win something, people believe in you.

Q: Goalies have reputations of being off-the-wall, yet you seem normal.

KW: They still go back to Glenn Hall having to throw up before games, Jacques Plante knitting toques and stuff like that. We've got a tough act to follow when we've got guys like that ahead of us. But, there's a few guys now that are a little quieter. They have to concentrate, that's the way they get themselves ready for games. When I first played with Peter Sidorkiewicz, he wouldn't talk to anyone the day of a game. He'd say the odd word to me at first. It took a couple of years, three years playing with him to where he finally just said, "Forget it. I'm just going to relax. I'm not going to tie myself in knots. It's not worth it." Kirk is the other end. He doesn't get excited about anything. He's just so relaxed and that attitude has helped me. I watch him play and I try to take that attitude out there when I'm on the ice. If he's sitting on the bench, we'll make a smart ass remark to each other while we're playing just to keep it light.

Q: I had heard that you and Kirk McLean once were trying to stay loose and had a contest to see who could stick the most sticks of gum in his mouth at one time. You said that Kirk could stick 51 sticks of gum in his mouth at one time.

KW: That was a thing that we had going in 1992-93 where we kept beating each other by one stick of gum.

Q: So it is true?

KW: Yeah, I don't know why he'd deny it. He didn't want anyone to think he had that big a mouth, I guess.

Q: So how many sticks of gum did you get in?

KW: Close to 60. Wrigley's. My mouth isn't very big. I was drooling. The gum was falling out of my mouth.

Q: It sounds like there's the two of you who sit off in this corner and then the rest of the team is somewhere else in the room.

KW: On game nights, that's how it is. We sit there and talk about which guy on the team is going to do what. We watch their rituals. A lot of guys have so many superstitions. Every guy says the same thing before the game and there's so many clichés. We just sit there and say, "Uh, oh. Guess what's coming next. Here comes the dump it in, dump it out," kind of thing. Some guys slap your stick in the same place and they lay their stick a certain way or they put their tape and their socks on a certain way. It's actually hilarious when you catch one guy who's got a whole bunch of superstitions.

Q: Talking to you, talking to Glen Hanlon and Kirk McLean, I get the impression that goaltenders are the only normal guys on the team. Glen was telling me that when he was on the ice he had this guy coming up and whacking him on the pads and another guy bonking him on the head.

KW: Right. All you have to do is watch the pre-period ritual every game and you'll know what we're talking about. All we do is stand there. You get a guy who comes in there and he has to hit your right foot, your left foot, your right hand, your left hand and tap you on the head before he goes off. That's not normal.

Q: I understand that you are quite a cook. Is that how you relax?

KW: Yeah. You eat on the road so many times and to eat something crappy at home wouldn't be good. I was lucky — I had the best cook in the world, my mom, when I was growing up. She put all my favorite recipes into a book when I went to play pro my first year. I was living with these three guys in this big house and someone had to cook. So we tried these things. Over the years, I got pretty fond of it. I enjoy it. As long as there's a recipe I can pretty well figure it out. Pastas, and I do good things with steaks and chicken. I'm fond of my wok. I live right downtown by the market so I just go over there and buy everything fresh. Take the little boat back home, cook it all up. Have a two-hour meal. I love sitting there and preparing it. Actually, it's more fun cooking it than eating it, most of the time.

-26-
Chris Terreri

For most of his NHL career, Rhode Island-born Chris Terreri was known as "The Other Goalie."

He was invariably cast in the second-fiddle role, dating back to 1988-89 when he understudied for Sean Burke.

Even in the 1992-93 season, when it appeared that Terreri had a lock on the New Jersey Devils crease, backup Craig Billington emerged as a competent enough alternate to cause Terreri to look over his shoulder with concern.

When at last Billington was dealt to Ottawa, it appeared that the job was Terreri's, no questions asked. The feeling was reinforced when second stringer Peter Sidorkiewicz showed up at the 1993-94 camp with a damaged shoulder, leaving only rookie Martin Brodeur to occasionally spell the 29-year-old veteran Chris.

As Terreri's luck would have it, Brodeur starred from the outset and instantly became New Jersey goaltender 1-A. Not that this is all bad for the 5'8", 160-lb. Terreri. He has demonstrated his competence over seven years while ripening into one of best American-bred goaltending products since Frankie Brimsek.

After a mid-season practice, reporter David Levy sat with Chris and gleaned some of Terreri's thoughts on life and goaltending.

Q: Tell what your parents felt about you playing hockey.

CT: They were always supportive in anything we did. I played baseball, hockey, soccer. They took us everywhere. I can't say enough about that. Early practices, games all over New England. Back then, I guess there was no limit to the number of games you can play. We used to play, oh God, I remember when I was ten years old, 75 games, All-Star Olympics, travel team games, house league games. I played over 100 games when I was ten years old.

Q: When did you become serious?

CT: My friends and I grew up together in the same city, but there were three different high schools and one private school, and a lot of them ended up going to private school and they wanted me to go there, but I didn't. I went to one of the public high schools in my town and we were Division II. It's where my brothers and sisters went to school and I just followed, and if I was good enough to get a scholarship, fine.

Q: Is that what you were shooting for?

CT: Well, you weren't shooting for that. But I guess in junior or senior year in high school, you realize you have a chance to get a scholarship. If you were good enough to make it, it didn't matter where you were going to play.

Q: So what did you do to get that scholarship?

CT: I was fortunate. My high school coach was a good college player and a real good coach. In fact, he'd get me out there early before the team and work on shooting drills. He was real influential in making me work hard and he saw the potential. He pushed me as far as he could.

Q: How'd you get to college?

CT: My high school coach, Wayne Gaffney, went to PC [Providence College] and talked to the coaches, Bob Bellemore and Louie [Lou Lamoriello] and said, "Come take a look at him." I had some other schools look at me. Someone told me I couldn't go to prep schools and play because I wasn't that big. I just felt that I was ready academically, and I went to Providence on scholarship.

Q: Going back to Providence, tell me a little bit about Lou Lamoriello, how he's been supportive here and how it all worked out.

CT: It's unusual. He's was my coach in college my freshman year, then he became athletic director there. It was weird because I was drafted while he was actually coaching at Providence College. Then I came here and he helped with my first contract with New Jersey. Then a year and half later he's my boss. I've seen him from all ends of the spectrum. We have a good working relationship. He has his job to do and I have my job to do. He's always been supportive of me. I'm the first to know if I don't do my job then I'm not going to play.

Q: Tell me about Final Four Fever and being a Hobey Baker finalist.

CT: It's different, the playoffs in the NHL. This is your job. It's different in college because when you're in college there's that whole atmosphere. That's it, there's no other world around you. When you're in the NHL, now it's your job, it's how you make a living. You are professional. You are going to go out there and perform. It's fun, don't get me wrong. It's just a different atmosphere, it's a different way of looking at it.

Q: I see Jacques [Caron, the Devils goaltending coach] talking to you a lot at the morning skate.

CT: Yeah, that's the most important thing at this stage. I don't how much more refined you get your skills at a certain point. Certainly you can always keep improving, but it's hard to make big advances. You're not going to come to a major breakthrough. You're just going to maybe improve on the little things. That's why the mental side is so important.

Q: Jacques [Caron] has a "less is more" goaltending philosophy, where he feels the reason why you improved is because you're doing a lot less motion and you're more focused.

CT: The focus is a big thing for me. I think when I lose my focus my game falls apart. I've been able to stay more focused or focus better game-in, game-out as the years have progressed. That's a combination of maturity and coaching, and certainly the style of hockey our the team plays now. So much of your goaltending revolves around your team and that [style] becomes critical.

Q: You've had a lot of coaching changes the past three years. What is the difference with Jacques Lemaire, as opposed to other coaches you've had?

CT: Different philosophies. The one thing that Lemaire brought with him is the work ethic and discipline. And the coaches have been honest from Day One. That's all you can ask from your coaches. It doesn't matter if they're going to be nice guys, if they're going to be hard on you. You just want consistency from them. A set system, a set way so you're not always changing, because then you're always missing a gear. That's what they brought. They're very consistent and they bring a winning tradition.

Q: How have different coaches treated you? Did some of them treat you a little differently?

CT: I don't have any complaints. There again, different coaches have different philosophies. Some think goaltending is just a mystery, you know, and some try to take an active role in it with a goaltending coach. I've gone from one end of the spectrum to the other. Herb Brooks tried to get right in your head. He was hands-on, whereas Jacques will give you his ideas but he lets Jacques Caron pretty much handle the goalies.

Q: Do you prefer Jacques [Lemaire] to the "hands-on"?

CT: I have a great relationship with Jacques. I like it the way it is now.

Q: Is it weird to be playing hockey for a living?

CT: No, because I tell you what, yeah we make a good living, but it's not going to last forever. We're here seven days a week. It's a job. If anyone thinks it isn't, they're wrong. It's certainly fun to play. It's fun to play in the games. It's fun to go out there. It takes its toll on you from a mental standpoint, knowing that you have a job to do and you have to do it every night. You just can't go out there and take nights off. Day in, day out. It's a job, just like any job in that respect. Certainly, it's probably more fun than a lot of jobs. I'll be the first one to admit that. But it's not what everybody makes it seem to be. You're not out partying every night. You see the hotel room, you see the hockey rink for the most part. People have a hard time understanding that. You're just trying to get through it and keep rested for the game.

Q: What do you do in the off-season or the down time, starting with college?

CT: I'm not big on skating in the summer. I don't really go on the ice till three weeks before camp. I'll play golf, but I'll work out. I'm in the gym pretty much every day, lifting and doing aerobics. I try to do other things that aren't hockey related. You've got to give your mind a rest. You just can't go at it 365 days a year. You'll burn out. That's just like anything else. I think it's good to get away and when you come back, you'll always be more focused.

Q: How would you describe your goaltending style?

CT: I used to be more helter-skelter and really go all over the place. I've learned to control myself a lot more. I rely on my reflexes when it comes to any situation. It's my biggest asset. I've become much more of an angle goalie. Not to the point where

I'm a pure stand-up goalie. I know I'm not. I'll always be a butterfly goalie to some extent. But you learn over the years what works and what doesn't work. What you can get away with and what you can't get away with.

Q: Jacques [Caron] has helped you tremendously I guess?

CT: Yeah, a lot with the little things. He really just helped me see some things in a different light but I never realized what was important that maybe is important.

Q: He mentioned things like breaking down the game in segments, thinking better before games.

CT: I think you'll find a lot of little tips and a lot of goaltending coaches will break a game down, I've always done that. I think he's helped me more with following the puck with my stick and seeing the puck come all the way to you instead of just letting it hit you. There's a difference between watching the puck all the way till you stop it, or just getting in the way of it. And seeing it go and knowing when it's going to hit you.

Q: Like an active mind?

CT: Yeah.

Q: When you started, I guess when you became serious about hockey as a career, did you realize that you had to work out all the time?

CT: After my first season pro.

Q: Were you out of shape?

CT: I wouldn't say I was out of shape. I was in shape. I just wasn't very big. And physically, you can't imagine what an 80-game season is until you've gone through it. You never go through it in college. It was a culture shock to me. It was a very tough year. So when I got away from a year and skated with the Olympic team, I was able to build up my strength, build up my stamina. It just changed my whole mental attitude. When I came back after that I was a different person. Now it doesn't faze me at all. You can play and play and play and really it doesn't take a toll on you.

Q: What is the typical goaltender relationship? Is it one of "friendly competition"?

CT: Yeah, but you'll find different people definitely get along differently. For a few years I played with Craig Billington. We were good friends. I wouldn't even call it friendly competition.

We were friends. We would help each other. You're not wishing bad things. You want to help each other do the best you can, because you both want to do your best. I think that's become more the norm. As guys get older it becomes a much more mature situation really.

Q: In the end, the bottom line is that you want to work together to win the Stanley Cup.

CT: Exactly.

-27-
Kelly Hrudey

Years after he retires there will be debates about Kelly Hrudey's status among the better NHL goaltenders. Some critics insists that had Hrudey ever played with a truly top-flight, defense-oriented team — à la Patrick Roy with Les Canadiens — Hrudey would be a future Hall of Famer.

As it is Kelly, over the years, has been saddled with mostly mediocre clubs. And in 1992-93, when Los Angeles cruised all the way to the Stanley Cup finals, it was Hrudey's stellar puck-blocking that enabled them to get that far.

Kelly has enjoyed other superb moments, especially the legendary Easter Sunday eve-Easter Sunday match on April 18, 1987 when he faced the Washington Capitals in a playoff game that lasted into a fourth overtime. Hrudey's acrobatics enabled the Islanders to win the game and the series.

Ever amiable, Hrudey sat for this interview with his friend — also the Kings practice goalie — Harris Peet, who doubles as a stand-up comic and journalist.

Q: How did you become a goaltender?

KH: Where I grew up in Edmonton, everybody plays road hockey and street hockey. It was the same with us and, being like most kids, I took turns playing all the positions. I played forward, defense and goalie, but I never really paid much attention to it. At the time, the dad of one of my friends knew that I was thinking of playing ice hockey and was undecided about what position I wanted to play. After watching us he said that it seemed like every time I was in the goal, the ball would hit me more often than the other kids, so I decided to give it a try on ice. The way things happened, he had given me real good advice.

Q: At what age did you get that advice?

KH: I must have been about 11, because once I finally made up my mind to play hockey, my parents made sure that I didn't go right into it. I just skated for a full year before I actually joined up. So I was 12 when I started organized hockey with no prior experience.

Q: When did you think you might be able to make a living playing goal?

KH: Because I had such a late start, being a pro didn't enter my mind for a long time, so I was a long way behind everybody else. It wasn't really until I was drafted by the Islanders, in 1980, that I really gave it a thought. Being drafted was a good clue that there was maybe some sort of living in it, and still it seemed far away at that point. I truly realized how close — but also how far away I was — in my first exhibition game I played in that 1980 training camp. I played against Chicago in an exhibition game and then I realized that I could make a living from this.

Q: Being drafted by the Islanders who were doing so well, did you find that frightening? Did you think that your chances of getting to the NHL were less than if you had been drafted by a worse team?

KH: Yeah, it seemed awfully difficult at the time. They had lost a lot of goalies there on the Island, when I was drafted. I remember going into my first training camp with seasoned goaltenders like Billy Smith, Chico Resch, Richard Brodeur and Rollie Melanson. With goaltenders of that caliber in front of me, I felt it would be an awful long wait until I might get an NHL opportunity. Looking back now, I realize that that wait was important for me. It has a lot to do with my longevity in the game.

Q: When you were younger and you were watching the game on TV, who were your favorite goalies?

KH: My number one goalie was Parent of the Flyers. I could hardly wait for *Hockey Night in Canada* on Saturday nights, so I could just marvel at every guy. There wasn't anyone I disliked or didn't cheer for. I was in awe of every goalie in the NHL.

Q: When you think back to April 18th, 1987, what's the first thing that comes to your mind?

KH: Winning! Everything is judged on that. Even though that was such a long, memorable, historic game, I think that it would not have had any special feeling for me if we had not won. I don't know what Washington's goalie Bob Mason thinks of the game, but for me it's just such a special feeling. Pat LaFontaine scored the winner for us and I can still feel that same sign of disbelief and everything, now as I did early that morning at Capital Center.

Q: After the game you said: "Don't ask me anything about the first five periods because I've forgotten already. I thought it was a dream. I never thought I could face 75 shots and let in two goals." Do you still have no memory of the first five periods?

KH: *(laughs)* Looking back, yeah, I do. I watch the game occasionally. The game was so different back then. It really was. I watch that game and see how easy it was to play goal back then. Every year the players seem to get better and better — and when you look back on, like a five-year period, the players are three times better than they were back then. Games like that are just special to be involved in.

Q: What doesn't the average fan know about playing goal, that if he did know, he would appreciate goaltenders more?

KH: The true athleticism that it takes and the mental make-up that is required. It's a falsehood that you have to be a flake or weird to play goal. You need mental concentration that no other position demands. That is the challenge of it all. And it really is challenging. I've been around almost a dozen years, yet I find goaltending more fun and challenging than ever only because I'm playing against myself. That's really what I do every night I'm in the nets.

Q: What percentage of your game is mental and what percentage is physical?

KH: I used to say that it was 85 percent mental. Now I can safely say it's in excess of 95 percent. It doesn't matter how I feel now in the nets; I can feel as if it's not even my own body. I can feel so horrible in goal there and still play well.

Q: To get back to that Islanders-Capitals overtime game in 1987, that was the fourth longest. Could you imagine playing any longer than that?

KH: No, I can't. I don't think you'll see many games like that again. Considering the talent level of all the newer players, now it seems like it's going to be virtually impossible to hold a team off for that long in overtime.

Q: There's a story about the longest overtime game in history [the six-period overtime game between the Montreal Maroons and the Detroit Red Wings, which Detroit won], that after about the third overtime period, the teams were so tired (and, of course, you didn't have Zamboni machines back then, so the ice was a mess), that the two teams were willing to flip a coin for a winner. Would you have been willing to do that?

KH: *(laughs)* Never! Never! I would rather lose than flip a coin.

Q: You mentioned that so much of your game is just playing against yourself, but are there certain opposing players that you're more aware of than others, or that you start thinking about longer in advance than others? How do you get ready for them?

KH: My preparation doesn't start on game day. It usually starts the night before the game, or the afternoon prior to the day before the game. It's just such a learning experience and you really have to keep a mental notebook on all the players and what they like to do in certain situations. The more talented goal scorers come to mind first, and it's just a battle to figure out certain players and that's the challenging part about it. You don't want the goal-scorers on the other team to score on you. You take pride in not letting them get their points. I take pride in taking that away from them. We have different rewards playing net, but it's really about stopping the goal-scorers.

Q: What's your favorite arena?

KH: Vancouver, because I love the city in general. It's my favorite city in the NHL. There are certain buildings that you feel almost like it's home and others that you just feel like it's torture to play in. Vancouver is my favorite city and Calgary ranks up there also. The worst, surprisingly enough, is Washington. Even after that memorable game, it's still a very difficult building to play well in. It's a strange feeling because there's nothing different about the arena that would bring feelings like that, but it's like every time we go there it's just . . . ugly.

Q: If a fan looks up your stats, what won't these numbers show that you would want them to know about you?

KH: I've never been asked a question like that. Some people might not understand this, but I don't care if I leave any sort of legacy, good, bad or otherwise. I want to go out there and do my best each and every game. I know and understand the game. We all come and go and we're all quickly forgotten. We're all heroes when we play and we're all quickly forgotten later on. I want to be as anonymous as anybody else. That's it.

-28-
Dominik Hasek

Czech-born Dominik Hasek was voted the best NHL goalie in the 1993-94 after having been second-stringer through his early pro career in Chicago, then Buffalo.

That Hasek could beat Grant Fuhr out for the top Buffalo job was a feat in itself, but under coach John Muckler, Hasek demonstrated that some of the world's best netminders learn their trade in Europe.

Dominik's finest hours occurred in Game Six of the opening 1994 playoff round between Buffalo and the New Jersey Devils. Hasek won the game 1-0 in the fourth overtime period.

Although Hasek's command of English still is somewhat limited, he agreed to be interviewed by Buffalo reporter Keith Drabik. Their exchange follows.

Q: You were born on January 29, 1965 in a city called Pardubice in Czechoslovakia. What is the town like? Is it a small town?

DH: Yes, it's a very small town. About 1,000 people live there.

Q: When did you get your first pair of skates?

DH: I was about five or six. My father gave them to me and I started skating in an indoor rink in town. I played on the only organized team we had in Pardubice. It's not like in Buffalo where there are many different local teams in each town. There are about 190 players that try out for that team. The first cut is about 150 players. They finally get down to about 30 players. I played with Frank Musil of Calgary on that team. We were pretty good. We won one championship and then won again in two years and had three consecutive championship wins.

Q: Why did you become a goalie?

DH: My father brought me home a pair of goalie pads when I was five or six years old. I haven't played any other position. At first I never cared to play professionally. I just loved hockey. It was my favorite game to play, the best sport. Eventually I was drafted by Chicago in 1983. I learned it from someone. They said that I was drafted. I didn't care. It made no difference to me.

Q: On your first visit to the United States, what did you think of the country?

DH: Nice country. Very big.

Q: You were named Czechoslovakian goalie of the year in 1986, '87, '88, '89 and '90, Czechoslovakian player of the year in 1987, '88 and '90, and Czechoslovakian First Team All-Star in 1988, '89 and '90. What did all these honors mean to you?

DH: They were wonderful. I had a great time playing in Czechoslovakia. I always wanted to be the best. That was my goal.

Q: In the IHL in 1990-91, you played 33 games with the Indianapolis Ice with five shutouts and a 2.52 GAA. Who was working with you, and did it help your game?

DH: I didn't have anyone working with me. The first time I had someone work with me was after I came to Buffalo. The Sabres goalie coach is Mitch Korn. But you can't teach goaltending. I was just told to hold my hand out (*makes motion with hand for catcher's glove*) and put my stick on the ice. I was disappointed playing in Indianapolis. I thought I had made the first team, Chicago.

Q: Your first NHL game was 1-1 tie at Hartford [Nov. 6, 1990].

DH: Yes. That was a big game for me.

Q: 1991-92 — you started with Chicago, along with Ed Belfour. You were sent to IHL in November and recalled two months later.

DH: I had thought about going back to Czechoslovakia. I was very upset. I thought I was playing well. I had offers to play in Germany and France. I called Mike Keenan and asked him to let me go but he said, "No way."

Q: In the 1992 playoffs you stopped Mario Lemieux four times . . .

DH: I was trying to play my best for the team. We were behind a couple of goals at the time and I made a couple of great saves. It was nice to play for the Stanley Cup.

Q: What are your feelings about Ed Belfour, who kept you from being number one in Chicago?

DH: He is a great goalie. He has proven that he's got it all. He isn't a goalie who has a good game and then has a streak of a lot of bad ones. He plays well every night. Every day he plays his best.

Q: How did it feel to beat out Grant Fuhr in Buffalo?

DH: It was great. That's why I am a goalie. I want to play a lot. It was nice to stay healthy, and if I am healthy I can play a lot of goal. But then it was bad when the newspaper says that I have the flu and everybody in the media gets worried. I feel confident, much more than in Chicago.

Q: The first great Czechoslovakian in the NHL was Stan Mikita. Do you remember him, or did you ever meet him?

DH: I knew his name, but, naturally, I never saw him play. He was much older than me. But I did meet him.

-29-

Vincent Riendeau

Teetering on the edge of stardom in St. Louis, Vincent Riendeau saw his once-promising career severely curtailed by injury and then subsequent trades to Detroit and Boston. Neither of the latter deals proved advantageous for the French Canadian.

In 1993-94, as a Bruin, he had an opportunity to make an impact when number one goalie Jon Casey faltered. While Riendeau showed flashes of his past quality play as a Blue, he never quite impressed the Bruins brass enough for them to employ him on a regular basis.

By the start of the 1994-95 season Riendeau, 28, was still seeking a significant NHL goaltending niche.

The likeable puckstopper exchanged views on his business with Detroit reporter Jim Ramsay.

Q: What was it like growing up in Quebec?

VR: Hockey was big time for us. It was everything. Every Saturday night everyone watched the Canadiens on TV. It stays cold for a long time so we had lots of ice. The cold has a lot to do with why hockey is so big there. Basically, we were in the hockey mood for eight months out of the year.

Q: Tell me about your family.

VR: I have a sister who used to coach hockey. She loved it. When she was 20 or 21, she coached Bantam hockey. My dad was a big fan of the game. Mom and dad always were there with their support watching me play and giving me a ride to all the games.

I started at five years old. The first time on the ice we skated around and my dad was the coach. There was no goalie and he asked who wanted to be the goalie and I raised my hand and that was it, I was a goalie from then on. That was it. A goalie for life.

Q: Who were the biggest influences in your life and why?

VR: I have to go with my father. He was the person I spent the most time with. My mother and father. My father for the sports part and my mother for the rest.

Q: Take a journey from St. Hyacinthe to the NHL and tell me
     about your stops along the way.

VR: I played minor hockey in the city of Drummondville, Quebec,
     all the way up to Junior A. I played Junior for Verdun my first
     year. The second year I was traded and refused to go to that
     team. I chose to play college Triple A instead. I was traded from
     the team I refused to play for to my home town team,
     Drummondville. I was then chosen in the draft by Montreal
     and played two years with Sherbrooke in the American
     Hockey League. Then I started my NHL career.

Q: How tough is it getting to the NHL?

VR: It is surely tough but you just can't think about that. You have
     to go out and enjoy the game and play hard. Take the game and
     enjoy it and if it happens, it happens. A young player at, say,
     nine or ten shouldn't be worried about being an NHL player or
     star. They should just have fun.

Q: What are the biggest differences between the AHL and the
     NHL?

VR: Everything is so much quicker in the NHL. It's at least one or
     two seconds quicker when things happen on the ice. The
     players are so much more skilled at everything they do.
     Everything is upgraded and players are more mature. Even
     though things happen quicker, the great players are able to
     slow the game to their pace.

Q: When did you first realize that you had the talent to make the
     NHL?

VR: In my third year of Juniors when I went to the Montreal
     Canadiens training camp. That's when I started thinking I
     could make it.

Q: You played one game for Montreal. What was it like the first
     time you walked into that dressing room?

VR: It was really impressive going into the Forum. Hockey is such a
     big thing in Montreal. Hall of Famers like Jean Beliveau and
     Rocket Richard are such a big part of that. You think about all
     the Stanley Cups they have won. You learn a lot from known
     winners.

Q: What do you remember about being a Montreal Canadien?

VR: I didn't get along at all with the coach, Jean Perron, because he
     refused to use me. Then we played in Calgary and we were

losing 4-0 at the end of the first period. It was an awful game and he threw me in and we lost 8 to 1. It was a game where we got blown out and afterwards he said to me, "You wanted your chance and that was it." It was a real bad experience.

Q: Since you are a French Canadian, how do you feel about Eric Lindros refusing to go to Quebec when he turned his back on Les Nordiques a few years ago?

VR: I don't think the big deal with Eric was about Quebec as such. I think it was about money. It wouldn't have mattered if it were Quebec, Winnipeg or other places, all he wanted was a big contract and he got it by doing what he did. I'm not agreeing with what he did at all. He shouldn't have picked on the French people. He shouldn't have said anything. He tried all the excuses he could to get what he wanted and he got it.

Q: You were traded to St. Louis in 1988 and to Detroit in 1991. Was the second time any easier than the first?

VR: No. I was really happy the first time to leave Montreal. They had Patrick Roy and he's still there and he's still the best goalie in the league. It gave me the chance to play in St. Louis. They only had Greg Millen and no other depth in goal. The second time around wasn't a good one when I got traded to Detroit. I was playing in St. Louis and when you're happy and playing you don't want to leave.

Q: Which was your favorite team when you were growing up?

VR: It has to be the Canadiens. They were always so good, and besides they were the only team they showed on TV.

Q: Did you have a favorite player?

VR: It had to be Guy Lafleur. He was the best of his time.

Q: What makes your position so special?

VR: It's not an easy position to play. The team can play well and you can still lose, or the team can play real bad but you can still pull out a couple of points for them. If the goalie is not up for the games, it really doesn't matter what the other guys do. Team success depends on the goalie.

Q: How do you feel about fighting in the NHL?

VR: It has to be there. Hockey is a contact sport and I don't want to see some little guy going after a big guy and look brave because of the rules. You're going to get mad at some players because of what they are doing, like giving you a cheap shot.

As long as fighting is not used as a main ingredient to win and it's just there and it happens, then it's a part of the game. We have seen the bad years where the Flyers used it to win. It's never going to be like that again. They bring the skilled players over from Russia and Europe, not goons, so I don't think you'll ever see goon hockey again.

Q: Rules to protect goalies are always being looked at. Have they gone too far or would you like to see more changes?

VR: They are good right now. You can't play the game and think about rules like that. That's when hockey gets boring. We saw that in 1992-93 with all the new rules in training camp. No one was playing the game; they were just worrying about the rules. When you have to start thinking on the ice, that's when the fans get hurt because you don't put on a good show. The rules are good right now; there's not too many injuries.

Q: Some say when a goalie's out of the net, he should be fair game. How would you respond to that?

VR: I guess those people never played hockey or goalie either. I don't see the big deal about the goalie going to play the puck. Why should the goalie be hit? It doesn't make any sense to me. It's pretty stupid. You can still force the goalie to make a bad play by going right at him. Why hit him? I don't see that.

Q: You had a severe knee injury in the 1991-92 season and missed 59 games. What do you remember about it?

VR: I remember everything that happened that night. My knee really hurt and I had never hurt my knee before that. It was like I had been shot through the knee. I remember most the disappointment because it took almost three weeks for them to find out what had happened. I didn't find out until I woke up from the surgery and they told me I would be out for six months. Even though I was disappointed in the trade, I still wanted to come to Detroit and prove I was a good goalie. When you're told you're done for the season, it's awful. That wasn't a good year at all. I never think about it now. The doctors did a great job and it's 100 percent now.

Q: Is there a certain fear element in playing goal?

VR: No. You can't think about that because if you do, you're done. That's the main thing. Once you start that, you're too old and you have to retire. You have to react and if the puck hits you high, that's part of it. If you get hit, you get hit. That's part of the game.

Q: How has the game changed since you've been in the league?

VR: It's changed for the best because of all the skilled players coming in. They bring the level of play much higher. It's better for the game and better for the fans. That's how we will get the U.S. TV contract. It's all skilled players now and they get to show their stuff. It's no longer just dump it in and chase. So, the NHL is doing well right now, doing everything to speed the game up and giving more of a chance to the skilled players. That's what the fans want to see and that's what we all want to see.

Q: Tell me what you think it would have been like playing goal without a mask.

VR: There's no way I would have ever done it! Now with my mask I don't think about getting hit, but without it I'm sure I would have. Those old-time goalies were different. They had to be different. They deserved everything they got. Those guys should have been paid millions for exposing their bare face to shooters like Bobby Hull and Frank Mahovlich.

Q: There is a great amount of pressure on a goalie. Describe what that pressure is like.

VR: Sometimes when things aren't going well, that's when it starts really building up. You don't just have the pressure of getting your game back together, you also have the pressure that you can cost your team the game. It's not like other players. If things aren't going well for a forward, he just works on certain things and it will eventually come back. When you're the goalie, it doesn't work like that. You still have to put the team first.

Q: What are some of the critical aspects of goaltending?

VR: You can't let the fans bother you. You have to remain level with your feelings. You're going to play well and you're going to play bad, but you have to remember all the goalies in this league are good. The only way you can have a good career is to not let those things bother you.

Q: Do you ever get cut by your mask?

VR: I've had my mask for several years. The helmet doesn't wear out, but you have to change the cage four or five times a year. You get a good shot there and you have to change it.

Q; What does a shot off the mask feel like?

VR: So far it's not been bad. I have never been hurt after being hit like that. I would actually rather have the puck hit me in the cage than in the shoulders. When you get hit in the shoulders early in the season, the bruises go away. Later in the season ,when you have been hit there a lot, they don't go away. Sometimes that's when you need a day off to let them heal.

Q: What is the toughest part of the goalie's job?

VR: After you have a real bad night, you have the ability to come back the next night and play a good game and forget about it. You'll have nights when you cost your team a game and you have to get back and play well right away.

Q: How important is skating ability to a goalie?

VR: It's as important as it is to any other player. We have to have good balance and be able to be quick on our feet, it's just a different stride. We have to work on it every day.

Q: How do you know when to stay in the net and when to come out?

VR: It all depends on your style. Some goalies like to stay deep all the time. If the guy's being chased and there's no way he can cut in and he's got his head down, that's a good time to go out and cut down the angle.

Q: How and what does a goalie communicate to his defenseman?

VR: When the puck is dumped into your zone, the defensemen are coming in and have their back to the play, so they can't see what's going on and you can. You have to tell him where the winger is or that he has a guy following him, or whatever is happening at the time.

Q: How do you prepare for a game?

VR: I don't have a routine. I don't like doing anything the same. It makes life boring. I hate for everyday to be the same. I like to do different things. I take the game as it comes. But after it's over, I take the game home with me all the time. I try not to, but sometimes I can't help it. You're concerned but you try not to talk about it. Everybody is the same, no matter how hard you try and not bring it home, you do. It's tough.

Q: In the 1992-93 season you only saw limited playing time. Did the adoption of your son Sam help you through a tough period?

VR: Actually, that happened at the end of the season and there was already a lot of frustration that had built up. The worst part was up until December, because I didn't think that was the way I was going to be used. Finally I realized that was the way it was going to be and it didn't bug me anymore. It was fun with our child coming home and it was a relief, but still the damage had been done.

Q: Expectations were high when you were with the Red Wings in 1992-93. Everyone had you in the finals or winning the Cup. Was that unfair?

VR: It was not unfair considering the power in that lineup. We had one of the top teams in the league. Usually there are at least seven or eight teams that have a good chance of winning, but in the end there are only two. It's a matter of peaking at the right time. Remember the one year Pittsburgh won, they had to win two seventh games to do it in overtime, so you can't say they were that much better than the other teams.

Q: What is team chemistry?

VR: It's when everyone on the team has the same goal. The thing is, everyone must have the same goal.

Q: If a goalie loses his confidence, what can he do to regain it?

VR: Work hard. Keep remembering the good game he has played and keep reminding himself how he has played in the past. You've just got to try as hard as you can to get out of the slump as quick as you can.

Q: How important is a goalie coach?

VR: A goalie coach is important up to a certain level. If a coach is there all the time, you end up with a coach for two guys and I think that's a lot. I'd like to see a goalie coach who comes in, say every two weeks, and gives you some drills. It is important to have someone to relate to but sometimes it can be too much.

Q: How do you feel about Manon Rheaume, the first female professional goalie?

VR: She has to be a great athlete. To me it doesn't make any difference if it's a woman or a guy. She is making a good name for herself in the sport. If she doesn't succeed as a goaltender, she will certainly succeed as a businesswoman. She is making the right contacts and if she wants to continue in sports she has put herself in a good situation. I'm sure she has gone through some difficult situations and her mental toughness has to be unbelievable.

Q: Do you know who is on the ice during a game?

VR: Yes you do. You have to. You know the players and what their strengths are. If not you're in trouble. I keep a "book" on players in the league but it's all in my head. You either played with them or against them and you know what they can do and when they like to do it.

Q: Do you watch videotapes of yourself after a good or bad game?

VR: No. I never do. I know exactly how the game went in my mind. I remember every goal and I don't need to see it on video; I can see it in my mind. The only thing I could use it for would be as a confidence booster by watching when I was playing very well.

Q: What is your relationship with your other goalie? In Detroit it was Tim Cheveldae. Did you talk to help each other?

VR: We didn't talk about hockey much. We talked about the team a little bit. We both knew what we had to do. There's not much you can do to help the other guy. We all know what it takes and we know our mistakes. Nothing is hidden in our position. When something is going wrong, you know it. You don't need the other guy telling you. You put enough pressure on yourself so you don't need anyone else adding to it.

Q: Goals-against average is used to rate a goalie. Is that an overrated statistic or not?

VR: It is a good picture, but you have to look at the overall game. When Grant Fuhr was with Edmonton he didn't have the best goals-against average but he was still the best goalie. It is important, but it has to be related to the overall team performance.

Q: You are always accessible to the media. How tough is it to face them after a bad game?

VR: It's tough but that's part of the game. You always like to talk when things go well, so you have to face them when it doesn't. You have one team who wins and one who loses; if you only talked to one team it would get pretty boring. You have to talk to both sides. Even if you lose, there are things that happen that are interesting. It's not always going to go well, but you have to be there to face it. People who cover the games have a big influence. They write something and the people who read it aren't here everyday, so they believe it. If you're being judged in the wrong way, people are still going to take what they read and that's how they are going to judge you.

Q: Are there ever times you just don't feel like coming to the rink?

VR: That happens often. Sometimes you are really physically tired and drained. Mentally also. Sometimes when things aren't going well you'd just like to go away for a couple of days. You work hard everyday but if you stay away too long you lose your habits. You try and come to the rink and have fun, but sometimes it's not that easy.

Q: Is the season too long and how would you like to see it change?

VR: We went from 80 games to 84 games, which is not a huge change. I don't think the 84 games are too much but they need to get the season over sooner. Ending in June is ridiculous.

Q: What is the funniest thing that has happened to you in hockey?

VR: The incident actually occurred during my first game in the Forum. I was playing against St. Louis and was about 19 years old. The coach had told me I wouldn't be playing that night so I was pretty relaxed and just watching the game. During the game he looks at me and says, "Do you want to go?" I said, "Sure." I had to run to the dressing room and get my equipment. In Montreal the bench area is pretty small. I went to jump over the boards and I tripped and fell face first. My first game in the Forum and 18,000 people were laughing at me. It was pretty embarrassing at the time but I had to laugh about it afterwards.

Q: Which cities have the best fans?

VR: St. Louis and Chicago. The fans in both places are unbelievable. St. Louis on a Saturday night is crazy. Both places have great atmosphere. People are there to yell and scream and have a good time. They want to see a good show and it puts you in a good mood. The worst fans are in Edmonton and Winnipeg. They don't say anything. Toronto is the same, except for the playoffs; sometimes it's so quiet it gets boring.

Q: I'll ask you some questions about who's the best and you give me a name and why: Mario Lemieux.

VR: It had to be Mario Lemieux in his prime. He slowed the game down. When he got the puck, everybody froze until they saw what he was going to do. He was amazing.

Q: Best goalie?

VR: It has to be Patrick Roy, but not far behind is Ed Belfour. Roy is the reason that Montreal has had a good team for the last four or five seasons. They had a good team for years; before that they had nothing.

Q: Hardest shot?

VR: You have to go with Brett Hull for the one-timer from the slot. Then you have Stephane Richer for the slapshot. Also, Al MacInnis.

Q: Best skater?

VR: Sergei Fedorov. He's really deceptive because he accelerates so quickly. For just flying I like Mike Modano when he puts on the jets. It's a different style, though. He goes fast when he takes off, but Sergei is quicker.

Q: Best passer?

VR: I would go with Adam Oates. He's a hell of a passer. And again, when he's healthy, Lemieux. He has to be there because he has done it for some time.

Q: Best stickhandler?

VR: It has to be Lemieux. He does whatever he wants with the puck. He's an amazing player but Stevie Yzerman isn't far behind.

Q: Best fighter?

VR: It has to be Bob Probert. He's the only guy I haven't seen other players challenge or yap at on the ice. Everybody respects him.

Q: What advice would you give a young goalie?

VR: Work hard and really focus on what you are doing. Don't let things bug you. And give yourself the best chance to succeed. Practice as much as possible.

Q: Do you have any hobbies?

VR: I do a lot of different things. I like to work on my computer. I have several businesses. I have my hockey school, some real estate things with my father. I'm interested in a lot of things. We took Spanish last year, our third language. I always like to keep busy and learn things every day. That's my goal.

Q: Should hockey players be role models for our youth?

VR: Sure. We're seen by the public all the time. It's important to behave, but it's also important not to hide things and just act like you're nice at certain times. It's important that people see the real you. Not everyone is the same and I like to see people be themselves. I like to see players say what they feel and I would like to see them express themselves more. Players would like to say more but it's tough. You say something and then someone criticizes you for it.

Q: What would you like to do when your career is over?

VR: I would like to be a teacher but I would have to go to school for three or four years, but that's something I wouldn't mind.

Q: Do you want to stay in hockey in some capacity?

VR: No. I'm not going to stay in hockey. That's going to be over with and I don't want to stay in any way. I have been playing hockey since I was five and I think it will be time to do something else. I would really hate myself if all I ever did in my life was hockey.

Q: How would you like to be remembered when you leave the game?

VR: From a fan's point of view, they will never really know me. They will just judge me by how I played on the ice. I would like to be remembered as someone who enjoyed the game, had fun and enjoyed his teammates.

Q: You said the fans only know the players from playing the game and that's a shame. Why?

VR: That's because of all the stardom people give you. It stops you from being able to let them know you. They put you on a different level and that is a shame. I would really like it if the fans could know me and the type of person I am. I enjoy people and like to talk to them. I like to hear what they have to say about everything. That's how we learn.

-30-
Darren Pang

In a relatively short big-league career, Darren Pang nevertheless carved a niche as one of the most likeable and competent goaltenders to come down the pike.

A member of the Chicago Blackhawks during one of their more successful periods, 1984-89, Pang was in the nets for one of the most stirring games in NHL history.

Facing the New Jersey Devils at Chicago Stadium in the final game of the 1987-88 season, the Blackhawks would have eliminated the visitors from a playoff berth with a victory. Until that point, New Jersey had never made the playoffs since the franchise was born.

In their desperate attempt at fourth place, the Devils poured volley after volley at Pang, finally forcing overtime. If the Blackhawks could force a tie, New Jersey would be out of it again.

As luck would have it, Pang made an excellent stop on a Joe Cirella shot but gave up the rebound and John McLean of the Devils slapped the puck past him for the game-winner and playoff-berth clincher.

Like many of his ilk, before and after, Pang was saddled with the "too small" label from his earliest years of goaltending right up to the NHL. It mattered not that some of the finest goaltenders through the years — Hall of Famers such as Roy Worters and Gump Worsley — were knee-high-to-a-grasshopper.

Pang successfully coped with the critics and was a serious candidate for the Calder Trophy as Rookie of the Year, only to be nosed out by Joe Nieuwendyk. Darren played capably for the Blackhawks until injuries and a new career opportunity induced him to pack in the pads.

He easily segued into the television world and became an NHL analyst for SportsChannel Chicago. Typically, Darren treated hockey with good humor and insight. His television work has been widely acclaimed, and in 1993-94 he was assigned by ESPN to cover the NHL All-Star Game and the Stanley Cup playoffs.

When Pang was at Madison Square Garden for the All-Star festivities, Stan Fischler interviewed Darren about his evolution as a netminder. Pang's odyssey follows.

Kids become goalies in funny ways, and usually stop becoming goalies when they take a hunk of rubber in the mush. With me it was the opposite. I started out as a forward and was standing in front of the net when a shot came right in front of me and hit me flush on the eye. My eye shut up and I walked back home to show my folks that I had a black eye.

So, why did I become a goalie? One day our team had a practice but our regular goalie didn't show up. The coach went the rounds asking each kid if he wanted to put on the pads but nobody raised his hand. My father, who had been a pretty good high school goalie, happened to be there. He raised his hand and said, "My son will give it a try."

Next thing I knew I was in the nets and a couple of weeks after that — at the ripe old age of six — I was put on the traveling team.

I loved it for a lot of reasons, but most important was the ice time. The other kids would be sitting on the bench, wondering when they were going to play — and for how long — while I stayed on the ice the whole time. And let me tell you, when you're a kid that means a lot.

Another thing I liked about it was the goalie's equipment, especially the pads. At the age of six, I had red-white-and-blue pads and a pair of Boston Bruins skates. Was that a color combination or what!

Now don't get the impression that I was a whiz-bang as soon as I got into the crease. Far from it. Once, a guy shot the puck from the other end of the ice and beat me. It was unbelievably humiliating; the worst feeling ever. I felt so bad I was crying and literally didn't think I could stop another puck again. I felt as if everyone was making fun of me — all 40 people in the stands.

But my dad supported me, and I was able to regain my confidence. Dad made sure that I had all the support I needed, including help from goaltending schools. I went to all the goalie schools and once won a Ken Dryden stick, which stayed on my wall for years. The joke is that when I got big enough, I began using the Dryden stick in games, something I never should have done because it already had become an important piece of memorabilia. I could kick myself for using it but I still have the beat-up stick to this day.

Dryden was one of my favorite goalies of all time, partly because I was a Montreal Canadiens fan. Even before Dryden, I loved Rogie

Vachon, who was the Habs top goalie before Dryden arrived. What I liked about Vachon was that he was such a little guy, just like me. When Rogie got traded to the Kings, I followed his career closely and was very pleased that such a small goalie could continue playing so well for so long. That gave me great encouragement.

I was also encouraged by my personal progress. As an early teenager, I was already playing with older guys and in 1979 was invited to play in the Air Canada Cup tournament in Cornwall, Ontario. I was playing with good competition and holding my own. Next thing I knew, I moved through the ranks and wound up in goal for the Ottawa 67s, the same team that sent Denis Potvin and Bobby Smith to the NHL, among others.

When I arrived in Ottawa, the coach Brian "Killer" Kilrea, asked me whether I was up for playing that very night. Obviously, he had his doubts about throwing me right in, but I said, pretty cocky, "Yeah, I should play!"

Well, we were outshot by a large margin that night, but I more than held my own and the club came out with a 4-3 win. Guess what? I was voted the first star of the game. Man, what a high that was. An hour later, we got on the team bus and I felt enormous. Here I was on a new team, in new surroundings and I had this tremendous confidence about me because I knew that I had climbed to a new level.

But that was just the start of something big. The next year was even better. What a team we had: future big-leaguers such as Adam Creighton, Gary Roberts, Brad Shaw with a great coach in Killer Kilrea. We won 13 games in a row to reach the Memorial Cup finals. Finally, I had one clinker; I got blown apart for seven goals and we lost 7-2, but Killer came back with me and we won the Memorial Cup.

It was around that time that I began to understand that I was being viewed as a "small goalie," and that it was said in a sort of derogatory way. Like small goalies really don't have that good a chance to go all the way. But that just strengthened my resolve to make it.

After the Memorial Cup, the Chicago Blackhawks signed me to a year contract with an option and they gave me a $2,500 signing bonus. With that, I took everybody out to dinner and the next stop was The Windy City.

My introduction to Chicago was not exactly something prepared by the chamber of commerce. We were bussed from our hotel to Chicago Stadium, which is located in a very seedy part of the city. Just as our bus pulled up to the arena, I noticed that five bodies were being taken out of a housing project across the street. You can imagine the looks on our faces as the bodies were carted away. I couldn't believe what I was seeing; I was bewildered.

Now I'm in camp only two days and somebody from the Stadium stole my wallet with all my immigration papers. What a start for training camp! Anyway, I didn't make the big club and wound up being sent down to Milwaukee of the International League. They designated me the second goalie behind Jim Ralph, but he got hurt so I ended up playing 56 games that year and got called up to Chicago in February 1985. I couldn't get over it. At the time the Hawks had two goalies, Murray Bannerman and Warren Skorodensky.

They dressed me for my first game but I didn't play. However, my size haunted me again. During the warmup, I was skating around the ice when my defenseman Doug Wilson sidles up to me and says, "Larry Robinson [of the Canadiens] stopped me in the warmup and asked me, 'Where is the other half of your goalie?'"

Finally, the game starts and right in the first period, Skorodensky pulled his groin. Maybe he should have been pulled from the game then and there, but he decided to stay in the net. Meanwhile, our coach Bob Pulford is getting worried. If Skoro gets hurt, it means that he has to put me in the net. I could see the look of fear in Pully's face. He must have been thinking, "What on earth have I gotten myself into?"

Pully figured he'd have to put me in sooner or later so he patted me on the back and said, "Get ready. Get ready."

Then, Skoro went down again and the trainer went out to see him but he got back up and continued playing. He stops a couple of shots and goes down, again! Skoro must have gone down seven times and insisted on staying in there. Meanwhile, I'm sitting on the bench thinking, "The longer Skoro stays in there, the more he's going to hurt his groin and the longer I'm going to stay in Chicago."

Sure enough, two nights later, I started in Minnesota. Pully gave me the word on the morning of the game and, right away, I got sick. I couldn't eat my food, I couldn't sleep. I was a mess and I couldn't believe that I was reacting that way. Then again, it was in the great Chicago goalie tradition. Glenn Hall, who played more than 500 straight games for Chicago, without a mask, used to throw up before every game.

And guess what? I began doing a Glenn Hall throughout my career. I'd lose my food before every single game. Honest to goodness. And never once was it done deliberately.

The routine would start the minute I woke up in the morning. I'd have a knot in my stomach and couldn't digest my food. This would last right up until game time, which was funny, in a way. In order to get myself to the bathroom at the Stadium, I would have to walk by my defenseman, Bob McGill, who was a real rah-rah guy. As I walked by, he'd be rallying the troops: "Pang is ready to go. Come on gang!"

Aware of my problem, the guys were trying to keep me loose before my opener in Minnesota. Finally, the game starts and we're all over the North Stars, but we couldn't score. Next thing I know, they've got the puck and began counterattacking. Just then, Pully made a line change, but it didn't synchronize very well.

What should have been a three-on-two break for them turned into a three-on-one, and they scored on their first shot at me. Some start.

Luckily, I was able to get back into the groove and began feeling great; except, of course, for the wise guys in the stands. One of them yelled out, "Hey, Pang, the Peewees are next for you!"

Anyway, as good as I felt, I couldn't win the game. We were down 2-0 at the end of the first and then they scored two power-play goals and it ended up being a 4-1 loss.

Still, Pully made me feel good after the game. He said he was very proud of the way I played. "You really did a good job," he said.

I felt pretty good about myself overall. Naturally, there were some blunders and my teammates had some getting used to in terms of my style. Like Doug Wilson had no idea how I handled the puck on the dump-ins by the opposition. What I liked to do was get the puck on my backhand, cradle it and then hoist it over everybody.

On this particular occasion, Doug was coming back for the puck and I thought he had seen me. I got to the rubber and, as usual, I hoisted it but the puck came this close to his nose and my stick came *this* close to his nose.

"What are you doing?" Dougie asked as he skated past me.

I said, "Heads up, Willy," and from that point on, my teammates knew that I played the puck a bit.

My debut, being that it wasn't a smash hit, got me no further games after that. I stayed up with the big club for a month but never got to play another game. Matter of fact, it was some time before I became an NHL regular, although I did get into an exhibition game the following fall at Chicago Stadium. We played the Edmonton Oilers and I started. Once, I stopped a two-on-one with Wayne Gretzky and Jari Kurri carrying for them. It was 1-1 at the time and the fans went nuts. Although I played well, they shipped me down to the minors again and I stayed there much longer than I would have liked, but my time in the bigs finally came and for that I say God bless Wayne Thomas.

He had once been a darn good NHL goalie and now was the Blackhawks assistant coach. Wayne kept telling me to get myself ready in the off-season, and that I would get a fair shot with the Blackhawks. That September I went to an early camp and Wayne honest-to-goodness went to bat for me. This time I made the team.

My first game was against Washington at Capital Center and, if nothing else, I maintained my tradition of not stopping the first shot. This time the Caps dumped the puck in and I took a gamble trying to clear it before Mike Gartner rushed in. Unfortunately, Gartner is one of the fastest skaters in the league and he got to the biscuit first, put it off my skate and into the empty net. Again!

Even though we lost the game, 6-4, they came back with me on home ice against Winnipeg and, this time, I got my first win, 6-4. And, yes, I still have the puck. This was quite a thrill, to be sure, but it certainly wasn't my best NHL moment. That one came when the Oilers had their powerhouse club in the late 1980s and we played them at Northlands Coliseum. They threw 54 shots at me and even though we lost, 4-3, I was picked the game's first star.

That game was a turning point for me and I settled in as a big-league goaltender after that. Once, I stopped a slapshot during a warmup and broke my finger. I talked them into letting me play and they taped up my hand and cut up my glove and we beat Edmonton 5-4.

One of the best parts of my career was the luxury of being able to play so many games in a special place like Chicago Stadium. This was an unbelievable experience because the fans there were so intense. And, let me tell you something: when Chicago fans like you — as they apparently liked me — they like you till the bitter end.

I might feel out of sorts before a game but by the time I had climbed those steps leading from the dressing room to the ice, I knew that I'd be able to respond just by the way the fans responded to me. I loved that building and I knew the boards, knew where the bounces would go. I knew that when I made a glove save, the fans would love it, and they did.

In 1987-88 I played in 50 games and suddenly became a candidate for rookie-of-the-year and a chance at the Calder Trophy. I knew that it wasn't going to be easy, because the Calgary Flames had a real hotshot shooter in Joe Nieuwendyk, who was having a helluva year.

Then, a funny thing happened: the producer of our SportsChannel Chicago telecasts, Lisa Seltzer, was a very inventive woman and a fan of mine. She knew that Nieuwendyk was my competitor for the Calder Trophy and she also knew that his name was almost impossible to spell correctly the first time around. And maybe the second and third as well.

So, Lisa came up with this bright idea. She had a whole bunch of T-shirts made up which were supposed to be sent to all the hockey writers who voted for the rookie-of-the-year award. On the front of the T-shirt, in bold letters, it said, "PANG IS EASIER TO SPELL THAN NIEUWENDYK."

Just about everybody in hockey got a big kick out of that and we went on a big campaign to get me those Calder votes but Nieuwendyk, to his credit, had 50 goals that year and he eventually beat me out for the prize.

That also was the year of the memorable final game of the season against New Jersey. The Devils came into Chicago having to win if they were to make the playoffs for the first time. But the game also had meaning to me. I figured that I'd be the Blackhawks starter in the upcoming playoffs and I wanted to get on a roll with a win against New Jersey.

One of our problems that game was emotion. We were stuck in third place with nowhere to go while the Devils were extremely pumped. They had something like 45 shots at me overall, and then came the overtime. Joe Cirella, their defenseman, took a shot for them and I stopped it with my stick but I couldn't control the rebound.

My old Junior nemesis from the Oshawa Generals, John McLean, got the puck and John always was one for the timely goals. Funny, I always really liked McLean because he could come up with the big one.

When he scored the goal, I was on one knee and the most vivid thing I remember about that episode was watching all the guys on New Jersey celebrating. I was very happy for them. I remember the joy on their faces and how Wayne Gretzky had once called the Devils a "Mickey Mouse" club.

But, most of all, I remember how happy I was for them.